Cleveland Amory is a distinguished American columnist and satirist and the author of several works of social history. In 1967 he founded The Fund for Animals in New York which campaigns against all forms of cruelty to animals throughout the world.

The Fund for Animals can be contacted at 200 West 57th Street, New York, USA.

THE CAT WHO CAME FOR CHRISTMAS

CLEVELAND AMORY

Illustrations by Meg Rutherford

BANTAM BOOKS
TORONTO · NEW YORK · LONDON · SYDNEY · AUCKLAND

A BANTAM BOOK 0 5531 7523 8

Originally published in Great Britain by
Bantam Press Ltd, a division of
Transworld Publishers Ltd

PRINTING HISTORY
Bantam Press edition published 1988
Bantam Books edition published 1989

Bantam Books are published by Transworld Publishers Ltd.,
61-63 Uxbridge Road, Ealing, London W5 5SA, in Australia by
Transworld Publishers (Australia) Pty. Ltd., 15-23 Helles
Avenue, Moorebank, NSW 2170, and in New Zealand by Transworld
Publishers (N.Z.) Ltd., Cnr. Moselle and Waipareira Avenues,
Henderson, Auckland.

Made and printed in Great Britain by
The Guernsey Press Co. Ltd., Guernsey, Channel Islands.

To the biographee,
the best cat in the whole world —
with the exception, of course,
of yours.

Contents

I · *The Rescue*   3

II · *The Decision*   19

III · *The Great Compromise*   34

IV · *His First Trip*   50

V · *His Roots*   71

VI · *A Difficult Matter*   91

VII · *His Hollywood*   114

VIII · *His Fitness Program*   145

IX · *His Foreign Policy*   175

X · *His Domestic Policy*   207

L'Envoi   238

The author wishes to acknowledge the help of his peerful editor, Fredrica Friedman, and his defatigable researcher, Susan Hall, as well as that of his severest critic, P. Bear.

The Cat Who Came for Christmas

I ∘ *The Rescue*

To anyone who has ever been owned by a cat, it will come as no surprise that there are all sorts of things about your cat you will never, as long as you live, forget.

Not the least of these is your first sight of him or her.

That my first sight of mine, however, would ever be memorable seemed, at the time, highly improbable. For one thing, I could hardly see him at all. It was snowing, and he was standing some distance from me in a New York City alley. For another thing, what I did see of him was extremely unprepossessing. He was thin and he was dirty and he was hurt.

The irony is that everything around him, except him, was beautiful. It was Christmas Eve, and although no one outside of New York would believe it on a bet or a Bible, New York City can, when it puts its mind to it, be beautiful.

And that Christmas Eve some years ago was one of those times.

The snow was an important part of it — not just the snow, but the fact it was still snowing, as it is supposed to but rarely does over Christmas. And the snow was beginning to blanket, as at least it does at first, a multitude of such everyday New York sins as dirt and noise and smells and potholes. Combined with this, the Christmas trees and the lights and decorations inside the windows, all of which can often seem so ordinary in so many other places, seemed, in New York that night, with the snow outside, just right.

I am not going so far as to say that New York that night was O Little Town of Bethlehem, but it was at least something different from the kind of New York Christmas best exemplified by a famous Christmas card sent out by a New York garage that year to all its customers. "Merry Christmas from the boys at the garage," that card said. "Second Notice."

For all that, it was hardly going to be, for me, a Merry Christmas. I am no Scrooge, but I am a curmudgeon and the word *merry* is not in the vocabulary of any self-respecting curmudgeon you would care to meet — on Christmas or any other day. You would be better off with a New York cabdriver, or even a Yankee fan.

There were other reasons why that particular Christmas had little chance to be one of my favorites. The fact that it was after seven o'clock and that I was still at my desk spoke for itself. The anti-cruelty society which I had founded a few years before was suffering growing pains — frankly, it is still suffering them — but at that particular time, they were close to terminal. We were heavily involved in virtually every field of animal work, and although we were doing so on bare subsistence salaries — or on no salary at all for most of us — the society itself was barely subsisting. It had achieved some successes, but its major accomplishments were still in the future.

And so, to put it mildly, was coin of the realm. Even its name, The Fund for Animals, had turned out to be a disappointment. I had, in what I had thought of as a moment of high inspiration, chosen it because I was certain that it would, just by its mention, indicate we could use money. The name had, however, turned out not only not to do the job but to do just the opposite. Everybody thought that we already had the money.

Besides the Fund's exchequer being low that Christmas Eve, so was my own. My writing career, by which I had supported myself since before you were born, was far from booming. I was spending so much time getting the Fund off the ground that I was four years behind on a book deadline and so many months behind on two magazine articles that, having run out of all reasonable excuses, one of the things I had meant to do that day was to borrow a line from the late Dorothy Parker and tell the editor I had really tried to finish but someone had taken the pencil.

As for my personal life, that too left something to be desired. Recently divorced, I was living in a small apartment, and although I was hardly a hermit — I had a goodly choice of both office parties and even friends' parties to go to that evening — still, this was not going to be what Christmas is supposed to be. Christmas is, after all, not a business holiday or a friends' holiday, it is a family holiday. And my family, at that point, consisted of one beloved daughter who lived in Pittsburgh and had a perfectly good family of her own.

On top of it all, there was a final irony in the situation.

Although I had had animals in my life for as far back as I could remember, and indeed had had them throughout my marriage — and although I was working on animal problems every day of my life — I had not a single creature to call my own. For an animal person, an animal-less home is no home at all. Furthermore, mine, I was sure, was fated to remain that way. I travelled on an average of more than two weeks a month, and was away from home almost as much as I was there. For me, an animal made even less sense than a wife. You do not, after all, have to walk a wife.

I had just turned from the pleasant task of watching the snow outside to the unpleasant one of surveying the bills when the doorbell rang. If there had been anyone else to answer it, I would have told them to say to whoever it was that we already gave at home. But there was no one, so I went myself.

The caller was a snow-covered woman whom I recognized as Ruth Dwork. I had known Miss Dwork for many years. A former schoolteacher, she is one of those people who, in every city, make the animal world go round. She is a rescuer and feeder of everything from dogs to pigeons and is a lifetime soldier in what I have called the Army of the Kind. She is, however, no private soldier in that army — she makes it too go round. In fact, I always called her Sergeant Dwork.

"Merry Christmas, Sergeant," I said. "What can I do you for?"

She was all business. "Where's Marian?" she asked. "I need her." Marian Probst, my longtime and longer-suffering assistant, is an experienced rescuer, and I knew Miss Dwork had, by the very look of her, a rescue in progress. "Marian's gone," I told her. "She left about five-thirty, saying something about some people having Christmas Eve off. I told her she was a clock-watcher, but it didn't do any good."

Sergeant Dwork was unamused. "Well, what about Lia?" she demanded. Lia Albo is national coordinator of the Fund for Animals and an extremely expert rescuer. She, however, had left before Marian on — what else? — another rescue.

Miss Dwork was obviously unhappy about being down to me. "Well," she said, looking me over critically but trying to make the best of a bad bargain, "I need someone with long arms. Get your coat."

As I walked up the street with Sergeant Dwork, through the snow and biting cold, she explained that she had been trying to rescue a particular stray cat for almost a month, but that she had had no success. She had, she said, tried everything. She had attempted to lure the cat into a Hav-a-Heart trap but, hungry as he was and successful as this method had been in countless other cases, it had not worked with this cat. He had simply refused to enter any enclosure that he could not see his way out of. Lately, she confessed, she had abandoned such subtleties for a more direct approach. And, although she had managed to get the cat to come close to the rail fence at the end of the alley, and even to take bite-sized chunks of cheese from her outstretched fingers, she had never been able to get him to come quite close enough so that she could catch him. When she tried, he would jump away, and then she had to start all over the each-time-ever-more-difficult task of trying again to win his trust.

However, the very night before, Sergeant Dwork informed me, she had come the closest she had ever come to capturing the cat. That time, she said, as he devoured the cheese, he had not jumped away but had stood just where he was — nearer than he had ever been but still maddeningly just out of reach. Good as this news was, the bad news was that Miss Dwork now felt that she was operating against a deadline. The cat had been staying in the basement of the apartment building, but the superintendent of the building had now received orders to get rid of it before Christmas or face the consequences. And now the other workers in the building, following their super's orders, had joined in the war against the cat. Miss Dwork herself had seen someone, on her very last visit, throw something at him and hit him.

When we arrived at our destination, there were two alleyways. "He's in one or the other," Sergeant Dwork whispered. "You take that one, I'll take this." She disappeared to my left and I stood there, hunched in my coat with the snow falling, peering into the shaft of darkness and having, frankly, very little confidence in the whole plan.

The alley was a knife cut between two tall buildings filled with dim, dilapidated garbage cans, mounds of snowed-upon refuse, and a forbidding grate. And then, as I strained my eyes to see where, amongst all this dismal debris, the cat might be hiding, one of the mounds of refuse suddenly moved. It stretched and shivered and turned to regard me. I had found the cat.

As I said, that first sight was hardly memorable. He looked less like a real cat than like the ghost of a cat. Indeed, etched as he was against the whiteness of the snow all around him, he was so thin that he would have looked completely ghostlike, had it not been for how pathetically dirty he was. He was so dirty, in fact, that it was impossible even to guess as to what color he might originally have been.

When cats, even stray cats, allow themselves to get like that, it is usually a sign that they have given up. This cat, however, had not. He had not even though, besides being dirty, he was wet and he was cold and he was hungry.

And, on top of everything else, you could tell by the kind of off-kilter way he was standing that his little body was severely hurt. There was something very wrong either with one of his back legs or perhaps with one of his hips. As for his mouth, that seemed strangely crooked, and he seemed to have a large cut across it.

But, as I said, he had not given up. Indeed, difficult as it must have been for him from that off-kilter position, he proceeded, while continuing to stare at me unwaveringly, to lift a front paw — and, snow or no snow, to lick it. Then the other front paw. And, when they had been attended to, the cat began the far more difficult feat of hoisting up, despite whatever it was that was amiss with his hips, first one back paw and then the other. Finally, after finishing, he did what seemed to me completely incredible — he performed an all-four-paw, ears-laid-back, straight-up leap. It looked to me as if he was, of all things in such a situation, practicing his pounce.

An odd image came to my mind — something, more years ago than I care to remember, that my first college tennis coach had drilled into our team about playing three-set matches. "In the third set," he used to say, "extra effort for ordinary results." We loathed the saying and we hated even more the fact that he made us, in that third set, just before receiving serve, jump vigorously up and down. He was convinced that this unwonted display would

inform our opponents that we were fairly bursting with
energy — whether that was indeed the fact or not. We
did the jumping, of course, because we had to, but all of
us were also convinced that we were the only players who
ever had to do such a silly thing. Now when I see, without
exception, every top tennis player in the world bouncing
like cork into the third set, I feel like a pioneer and very
much better about the whole thing.

And when I saw the cat doing his jumping, I felt better
too — but this time, of course, about him. Maybe he was
not as badly hurt as at first I had thought.

In a moment I noticed that Sergeant Dwork, moving
quietly, had rejoined me. "Look at his mouth," she whispered. "I told you they have declared war on him!"

Ours was to be a war too — but one not against, but
for, the cat. As Sergeant Dwork quietly imparted her battle
plan, I had the uneasy feeling that she obviously regarded
me as a raw recruit, and also that she was trying to keep
my duties simple enough so that even a mere male could
perform them. In any case, still whispering, she told me
she would approach the fence with the cheese cubes, with
which the cat was by now thoroughly familiar, in her
outstretched hand, and that, during this period, I apparently should be crouching down behind her but nonetheless moving forward with her. Then, when she had
gotten the cat to come as close as he would, she would
step swiftly aside and I, having already thrust my arms
above her through the vertical bars of the fence, was to
drop to my knees and grab. The Sergeant was convinced
that the cat was so hungry that, at that crucial moment,
he would lose enough of his wariness to go for the bait —
and the bite — which would seal his capture.

Slowly, with our eyes focussed on our objective, we moved out and went over the top. And just as we did so, indeed as I was crouching into position behind Sergeant Dwork, I got for the first time a good look at the cat's eyes peering at us. They were the first beautiful thing I ever noticed about him. They were a soft and lovely and radiant green.

As Sergeant Dwork went forward, she kept talking reassuringly to the cat, meanwhile pointedly removing the familiar cheese from her pocket and making sure he would be concentrating on it rather than the large something looming behind her. She did her job so well that we actually reached our battle station at almost the exact moment when the cat, still proceeding toward us, albeit increasingly warily, was close enough to take his first bite from the Sergeant's outstretched hand.

That first bite, however, offered us no chance of success. In one single incredibly quick but fluid motion, the cat grabbed the cheese, wolfed it down, and sprang back. Our second attempt resulted in exactly the same thing. Again the leap, the grab, the wolf, and the backward scoot. He was simply too adept at the game of eat and run.

By this time I was thoroughly convinced that nothing would come of the Sergeant's plan. But I was equally convinced that we had somehow to get that cat. I wanted to get over that fence and go for him.

The Sergeant, of course, would have none of such foolhardiness, and, irritated as this made me, I knew she was right. I could never have caught the cat that way. The Sergeant was, however, thinking of something else. Wordlessly she gave me the sign of how she was going to modify her tactics. This time she would offer the cat not one but two cubes of cheese — one in each of her two outstretched hands. But this time, she indicated, although she would push her right hand as far as it would go through the fence, she would keep her left hand well back. She obviously hoped that the cat would this time attempt both bites before the retreat. Once more we went over the top — literally in my case, because I already had my hands through the fence over the Sergeant. And this time, just as she had hoped, the cat not only took the first bite but also went for that second one. And, at just that moment, as he was midbite, Sergeant Dwork slid to one side and I dropped to my knees.

As my knees hit the ground, my face hit the grate. But I did not even feel it. For, in between my hands, my fingers underneath and my thumbs firmly on top, was cat. I had him.

Surprised and furious, he first hissed, then screamed, and finally, spinning right off the ground to midair, raked both my hands with his claws. Again I felt nothing, because by then I was totally engrossed in a dual performance — not letting go of him and yet somehow managing to maneuver his skinny, desperately squirming body, still in my tight grasp, albeit for that split second in just one hand, through the narrow apertures of the rail fence. And now his thinness was all-important because, skin and bones as he was, I was able to pull him between the bars.

Still on my knees, I raised him up and tried to tuck him inside my coat. But in this maneuver I was either over-confident or under-alert, because somewhere between the raising and the tucking, still spitting fire, he got in one final rake of my face and neck. It was a good one.

As I struggled to my feet, Sergeant Dwork was clapping her hands in pleasure, but obviously felt the time had now come to rescue me. "Oh," she said. "Oh dear. Your face.

Oh my." Standing there in the snow, she tried to mop me with her handkerchief. As she did so, I could feel the cat's little heart racing with fear as he struggled to get loose underneath my coat. But it was to no avail. I had him firmly corralled, and, once again, with both hands.

The Sergeant had now finished her mopping and become all Sergeant again. "I'll take him now," she said, advancing toward me. Involuntarily, I took a step backwards. "No, no, that's all right," I assured her. "I'll take him to my apartment." The Sergeant would have none of this. "Oh no," she exclaimed. "Why, my apartment is very close." "So is mine," I replied, moving the cat even farther into the depths of my coat. "Really, it's no trouble at all. And anyway, it'll just be for tonight. Tomorrow, we'll decide — er, what to do with him."

Sergeant Dwork looked at me doubtfully as I started to move away. "Well then," she said, "I'll call you first thing in the morning." She waved a mittened hand. "Merry Christmas," she said. I wished her the same, but I couldn't wave back.

Joe, the doorman at my apartment building, was unhappy about my looks. "Mr. Amory!" he exclaimed. "What happened to your face? Are you all right?" I told him that not only was I all right, he ought to have seen the other guy. As he took me to the elevator, he was obviously curious about both the apparent fact that I had no hands and also the suspicious bulge inside my coat. Like all good New York City doormen, Joe is the soul of discretion — at least from tenant to tenant — but he has a bump of curiosity which would rival Mt. Everest. He is also, however, a good animal man, and he had a good idea that whatever I had, it was something alive. Leaning his head toward my coat, he attempted to reach in. "Let me pet it," he said. "No," I told him firmly. "Mustn't touch." "What is it?" he asked. "Don't tell anyone," I said, "but it's a saber-toothed tiger. Undeclawed, too." "Wow," he said. And then, just before the elevator took off, he told me that Marian was already upstairs.

I had figured that Marian would be there. My brother and his wife were coming over for a drink before we all went out to a party, and Marian, knowing I would probably be late, had arrived to admit them and hold, so to speak, the fort.

I kicked at the apartment door. When Marian opened it, I blurted out the story of Sergeant Dwork and the rescue. She too wanted to know what had happened to my face and if I was all right. I tried the same joke I had tried on Joe. But Marian is a hard woman on old jokes. "The only 'other guy' I'm interested in," she said, "is in your coat." I bent down to release my prize, giving him a last hug to let him know that everything was now fine.

Neither Marian nor I saw anything. All we saw, before his paws ever hit the ground, was a dirty tan blur, which, crooked hips notwithstanding, literally flew around the apartment — seemingly a couple of feet off the ground and all the time looking frantically for an exit.

In the living room I had a modest Christmas tree. Granted, it was not a very big tree — he was not, at that time, a very big cat. Granted, too, that this tree had a respectable pile of gaily wrapped packages around the base and even an animal figure attached to the top. Granted even that it was festooned with lights which, at rhythmic intervals, flashed on and off. To any cat, however, a tree is a tree and this tree, crazed as he was, was no exception. With one bound he cleared the boxes, flashed up through the branches, the lights, and the light cord and managed, somewhere near the top, to disappear again. "Now that's a good cat," I heard myself stupidly saying. "You don't have to be frightened. Nothing bad is going to happen to you here."

Walking toward the tree, I reached for where I thought he would be next, but it was no use. With one bound, he vanished down the far side and, flashing by my flailing arms, tried to climb up the inside of the fireplace. Fortunately the flue was closed, thus effectively foiling his attempt at doing a Santa Claus in reverse.

When he reappeared, noticeably dirtier than before, I was waiting for him. "Good boy," I crooned, trying to sound my most reasonable. But it was no use. He was gone again, this time on a rapid rampage through the bedroom — one which was in fact so rapid that not only was it better heard than seen but also, during the worst of it, both Marian and I were terrified that he might try to go through the window. When he finally materialized again in the hall, even he looked somewhat discouraged. Maybe, I thought desperately, I could reason with him now. Slowly I backed into the living room to get a piece of cheese from the hors d'oeuvre tray. This, I was sure, would inform him that he was among friends and that no harm would befall him. Stepping back into the hall, I found Marian looking baffled. "He's gone," she said. "Gone," I said. "Gone where?" She shook her head and I suddenly realized that, for the first time in some time, there was no noise, there was no scurrying, there was no sound of any kind. There was, in fact, no cat.

We waited for a possible reappearance. When none was forthcoming, obviously we had no alternative but to start a systematic search. It is a comparatively small apartment and there are, or so Marian and I at first believed, relatively few hiding places. We were wrong. For one thing, there was a wall-long bookshelf in the living room, and this we could not overlook, for the cat was so thin and so fast that it was eminently feasible that he found a way to clamber up and wedge himself behind a stack of books on almost any shelf. Book by book, we began opening holes.

But he was not there. Indeed, he was not anywhere. We turned out three closets. We moved the bed. We wrestled the sofa away from the wall. We looked under the tables. We canvassed the kitchen. And here, although it is such a small kitchen that it can barely accommodate two normal-sized adults at the same time, we opened every cupboard, shoved back the stove, peered into the microwave, and even poked about in the tiny space under the sink.

At that moment, the doorbell rang. Marian and I looked at each other — it had to be my brother and his wife, Mary. My brother is one of only three men who went into World War II as a private and came out as a colonel in command of a combat division. He was, as a matter of fact, in the Amphibious Engineers, and made some fourteen opposed landings against the Japanese. He had also since served as deputy director of the CIA. A man obviously used to crises, he took one look at the disarray of the apartment. In such a situation, my brother doesn't talk, he barks. "Burglars," he barked. "It looks like a thorough job."

I explained to him briefly what was going on — and that the cat had now disappeared altogether. Not surprisingly, while Mary sat down, my brother immediately assumed command. He demanded to know where we had not looked. Only where he couldn't possibly go, I explained, trying to hold my ground. "I don't want theories," he barked. "Where *haven't* you looked?" Lamely, I named the very top shelves of the closet, the inside of the oven, and the dishwasher. "Right," he snapped, and advanced on first the closets, then the oven, and last the dishwasher. And, sure enough, at the bottom of the latter, actually curled around the machinery and wedged into the most impossible place to get to in the entire apartment, was the cat. "Ha!" said my brother, attempting to bend down and reach him.

I grabbed him from behind. I was not going to have my brother trust his luck with one more opposed landing. Bravely, I took his place. I was, after all, more expendable.

Actually, the fact was that none of us could get him out. And he was so far down in the machinery, even he couldn't get himself out. "Do you use it?" my brother demanded. I shook my head. "Dismantle it," he barked once more. Obediently, I searched for screwdriver, pliers, and hammer and, although I am not much of a mantler, I consider myself second to no one, not even my brother, as a dismantler. My progress, however, dissatisfied my brother. He brushed me aside and went over the top himself. I made no protest — with the dishwasher the Amphibious Engineer was, after all, at least close to being in his element.

When my brother had finished the job, all of us, Mary included, peered down at the cat. And, for the first time since my first sight of him in the alley, he peered back. He was so exhausted that he made no attempt to move, although he was now free to do so. "I would like to make a motion," Marian said quietly. "I move that we leave him right where he is, put out some food and water and a litter pan for him — and leave him be. What he needs now is peace and quiet."

The motion carried. We left out three bowls — of water, of milk, and of food — turned out all the lights, including the Christmas lights, and left him.

That night, when I got home, I tiptoed into the apartment. The three bowls were just where we had left them — and every one of them was empty. There was, however, no cat. But this time I initiated no search. I simply refilled the dishes and went to bed. With the help of a Sergeant, a colonel, and Marian, I now had, for better or for worse, for a few days at least, a Christmas cat.

II ∘ *The Decision*

I awoke early the next morning — the earliest I could remember since the Christmas mornings of my childhood. In those days my brother and sister and I were allowed whenever we woke up to open our stockings with their presents inside, all individually wrapped and dutifully stuffed by Santa Claus. It was one of the few times I envied my sister. She not only still believed in Santa Claus — my brother and I were under threat of receiving no stocking at all if we attempted to persuade her otherwise — but she was also given a grown-up girl's stocking that was more than twice as long as ours and thus held many more presents. Liberation came early to our family.

In any case, my standing Christmas morning record for those days was 4 A.M. On my first Christmas with the cat, I did not break that record, but I came pretty close. Nonetheless, I decided to get up immediately and conduct a search for him. But, as I sat sleepily up in bed, I saw immediately that there would be no need for this. For, only a few feet from my bed, standing in almost exactly the same position he was in the first time I ever saw him, and looking straight at me in almost exactly the same way, was the cat.

He had evidently been standing like that for some time, waiting for some signs of life from me. Now, seeing same, he spoke. "Aeiou," he said. "Ow yourself," I replied; "Merry Christmas." I reminded him that he was supposed to say "Meow." "Aeiou," he repeated. Obviously, he was not very good at consonants, but he was terrific at vowels.

As I got out of bed and walked close by him on my way to replenish his bowls, I noticed that he made no attempt to move away. Neither did he after he had finished eating and drinking. He just stood for a moment or two, licking and contemplating things. Then, slowly and solemnly, he began a tour of the apartment. When he went back into the bedroom, I followed him. In the corner, between the two windows, he paused and looked back at me. "Aeiou," he remarked once more. Obviously he wanted to get up on the windowsill and look out. And, equally obviously, this time he required some assistance, although the night before he had managed the same jump without any assistance — and at about thirty miles an hour.

I went over and lifted him. He looked around at me as I touched him but otherwise did nothing. Instead, after a moment, he continued his slow, solemn tour, this time of the windowsill. He spent some time looking down on the street below and out at the snow-covered Central Park.

Then he proceeded to jump across to the next window, which opens on a small balcony. This he regarded with such special interest that for some time he lay down, quietly moving his tail back and forth. He had, clearly, seen pigeons. Finally, he jumped down again and went back into the living room.

Once more I followed him and, for the very first time since I had seen him, he stretched out full length. Then he rolled over, put his head half under his shoulder and looked at me, meanwhile once again quietly moving his tail. Cats talk with their tails, and no cat ever expressed himself more clearly. "I'll take it," he was saying, in exactly the way a prospective new tenant, who had just made a complete tour of the premises, would agree to a lease. Satisfied, I went back to bed.

At about eight o'clock, the telephone rang. I could not believe anyone would call so early on Christmas morning. It was, as I might have guessed, Sergeant Dwork. "Merry Christmas," she said. "How's our cat?" "Fine," I replied, "just fine." I did my best to conceal the fact that, even at that stage of my life with the cat, I was not entirely happy with the "our." Apparently, I succeeded, because Sergeant Dwork went into high gear. "I've got great news," she said. "I have a woman who wants him."

"Terrific," I said. I did not, however, say this with enthusiasm, something Sergeant Dwork must have sensed, because she quickly added, "I know her and she'll give it a great home."

I told her I was sure she would. "But the thing is," Miss Dwork continued, "she wants it right away. She wants it as a Christmas present for her daughter. They lost their own, you know."

I didn't, of course, but I tried to mobilize, if not enthusiasm, at least acquiescence. When could they come and see it? Perhaps in the afternoon?

"Oh, no." Sergeant Dwork sounded shocked. "Not this afternoon. This morning. Right now. In fact, she's already on the way to your apartment. Her name, by the way, is Mrs. Wills."

"Whoa," I told her sternly. "Not so fast." I glanced to where the cat had settled himself at ease in the living room. "He's so dirty," I said, "and it seems so awful to move him again, just when he's beginning to . . ."

But Sergeant Dwork cut me off. "Nonsense," she said. "The sooner the better. If he makes himself too much at home with you — and you get too fond of him," and here a distinctly disturbing note crept into her voice, "well, it will be just that much harder for both of you when you do give him up. And, remember, you yourself admitted that a permanent animal made no sense at all for you, with the amount of time you're away and everything."

What she said, of course, did make sense, and I admitted as much. "Okay," I said, "I'll see Mrs. Wills. I'll call you afterward to let you know if she likes him."

As I hung up the phone, however, I could not look at the cat, although I could feel he was looking at me. Instead, I turned my head and looked out the window.

In short order, the doorbell rang. Mrs. Wills was a nice woman, but she was also a formidable one, and I am not at my best with formidable women early in the morning. Quickly I realized, however, that I was perhaps being unfair — one thing which made her seem so formidable was that she was carrying a large cat carrier.

"I'm sorry to be so early," she said briskly, as, in all senses of the phrase, she moved in, "but I wanted it for . . ."

"I know," I said, "for a Christmas present for your daughter." I turned to gesture toward the cat. But there was, of course, no cat.

"That's funny," I hedged. "He was here just a second ago." I looked around nervously. The thought of another search such as the one the night before and watched by Mrs. Wills had all the appeal of an IRS audit. Mrs. Wills looked around.

"Whatever happened in here?" she asked. "It looks as if you've been bombed. Did the cat . . . ?"

I had of course completely forgotten the total disarray of the apartment. "Oh the cat," I repeated, attempting a light laugh. "Oh no. It wasn't the cat. It was my brother. You see, my brother was here last night and we were looking for a book we couldn't find. My brother is a great reader, you know."

In explanations like that, one always adds one ridiculous note. Mrs. Wills' eyebrows rose slightly, as she surveyed the contents of the living room closet, which were still strewn across the foyer floor. "Hmmm," she said.

I asked her if I could get her some coffee. She shook her head. She obviously wanted only that for which she had come.

There was nothing to do but bite the bullet. "Here, boy," I boldly called, feeling not only idiotic, but knowing full well that the odds against his even being curious enough to acknowledge such a call, let alone come to it, especially with a stranger there, were astronomical. Nonetheless, I moved around the room, continuing my call while ostensibly straightening things but actually surreptitiously looking for him. Finally, just as Mrs. Wills had begun to tap her foot meaningfully, I maneuvered myself into the position I had first wanted to be in — i.e., pretending to straighten the rug by the sofa but actually looking underneath it. And there, sure enough, at the very back, against the wall, crouched and rigid, was the cat. "Oh!" I exclaimed, getting down on my hands and knees, "There he is! In his favorite place!"

Reluctantly, Mrs. Wills too assumed the position. "I can't see a thing," she complained. "Well," I volunteered, "I'll get a flashlight."

When I returned and shone the light upon him, his eyes glowed. The rest of him, however, had the look of a cornered hyena. "Oh," said Mrs. Wills. "Oh my. He's so wild-looking." "Oh, don't worry about that," I assured her. "He's just a little surprised."

"And he's so *dirty*," she went on. "Well," I answered stiffly, "remember, he's been a stray. On the street. He can be cleaned up in no time."

But the inspection was not finished yet. "Why is he crouched so crookedly like that?" she wanted to know. "Is there something wrong with him?"

"Oh that's nothing," I assured her. "He sometimes even stands like that. I'm sure it can be fixed. And anyway, remember, he's not really himself. He's nervous with both of us looking at him like this."

Mrs. Wills, however, was by now relentless. "There's something wrong with his mouth," she observed.

"He's got a cut," I replied. "A very little cut. Really just a tiny cut."

She maneuvered herself upwards and returned to her chair. "Oh dear," she said, as if talking to herself. "I really don't know. Now that I've seen him I'm really not sure.

I suppose I could try it. But Jennifer is just a little girl and this cat is going to take an awful lot of work."

I told her that I didn't think it would be that much. I had a suggestion for her. Why didn't she let me get him cleaned up and quieted down and then she could make her decision? I had in mind at least a couple of days.

The idea appealed to her — but not the timing. It had, apparently, to be a Christmas cat or no cat at all. She consulted her wristwatch. "I'll come back after church," she decided. "I'll leave the carrier here."

So, I reflected, that was that. I had at least tried to do what I thought would, in the long run, be the best thing for the cat. And while I realize that I could have acted a good deal more enthusiastic about the final outcome, the problem was that I just didn't feel very enthusiastic.

In any case, now there was nothing for it — Christmas morning or no Christmas morning — but to give him a bath. I went into the bathroom to procure soap and wash-cloths, over which I ran warm water, as well as a bath towel and even a bath mat.

When I returned to the living room, the cat was no longer under the sofa. He was back in the middle of the floor, just where, pre–Mrs. Wills, he had been before. It seemed to me that he understood exactly what the mat and the towel and all the rest of the paraphernalia were about, and knew exactly what I was about to do. But, at the same time, it also seemed that he simply could not believe I would do such a thing. His tail made an incredulous rat-tat. "Wash a cat!" he was exclaiming. "Boy, have I got my work cut out for me with this one!" He clearly felt that whatever my inexperience and limitations as a cat-keeper might be, surely even I would be familiar with the basics — and what could be more basic than the plain and simple fact that washing was his job, not mine?

He rose to his paws and looked up at me. I looked down at him. We were, in a sense, eyeball to eyeball — I at six feet three and he at six inches. Just the same, it was going to be, as it always is in such a confrontation, a question of who blinked first. And that would not, I had already determined, be me.

And it was not, really. All right, certain purists might cavil that I did not get right down to the job. They might even argue that I made a small blink. But they would be absolutely wrong and it would be utterly unfair to me to make any more of it than that. What actually happened is that, just at the moment when I was about to commence operations, and as his tail began to rat-tat ever more ominously, I suddenly decided, and quite on my own, having nothing to do with the fact that his back was slowly arching and he was making his ears flat, that it was entirely possible I didn't know enough about cat-washing, and should consult authorities.

Hastily, I laid down my washing materials, and repaired to the bookcase, where I had a whole shelf of books about cats. Like the other books, these were now in a state of sad disarray. Besides, I was looking for something very specific — not cats in general, but cat-washing. There were many references to the subject in the various book indexes, but as happens so often with thorny issues, there were also many disagreements. There were, in fact, two diametrically opposed schools of thought. One of these schools held that you should never, ever, wash a cat. The theory had it that not only do cats prefer to do the job themselves, but they also do it better than a human ever could, and furthermore, humans were likely to get soap in their eyes or in their fur, and this could be very bad for them. On the other hand, the other school believed that it was perfectly all right to wash your cat, and indeed was so essential that if you didn't, all sorts of bad things could happen to him.

I decided in view of the current situation, and weighing all the factors, to adhere to Theory Number Two, and thumbed through the books until I found one, entitled simply *You and Your Cat*, which seemed the most definitive on the subject. It was written by an English veterinarian, David Taylor, and, with high optimism, I began to read:

> The kitchen sink will probably make the best "bath." Before you start, make sure all the doors and windows are closed and that the room is free from cold drafts. Place a rubber mat in the sink to stop the cat from slipping.

So far, I decided, so good. The next paragraph, however, was another story:

> If you think your cat is going to struggle, put it in a cotton sack, leaving only its head visible. Pour the shampoo into the sack and lower the cat and sack into the water. You can then massage the cat through the sack and form a lather.

Put the cat in a sack! Maybe, I thought, my brother and his regiment could achieve that objective, but that I alone could do so was highly doubtful. True, the cat was quiet that morning, but remembering the whirlwind of the night before, and not being an Amphibious Engineer myself, I foresaw the possibility of something on the order of, if not Gallipoli, at least Dunkirk.

Nothing, however, stopped the aquatic advance of Dr. Taylor:

> Fill the sink with about 2–4 ins. of warm water. The water temperature should be as close to your cat's body heat of 101.4 F as possible. To lift the cat in, put one hand under its hind quarters and hold the scruff of its neck with the other. If your cat prefers, allow it to rest its front paws out of the water.

I was sure that the cat in question would not only so prefer, but would also seize the first opportunity to have a go with those paws at the alleged perpetrator of any such proposed ablutions. In any case, I had had enough. I replaced the book, went back to the cat, gathered up my materials, and with all the authority I could muster, spread the bath mat down beside him.

To my amazement, he promptly stepped over and stood upon it. Although I had taken the precaution of remaining standing for, if need be, a fast getaway, I soon realized that I had underestimated him. He had, apparently, made his point, but he had no intention of being churlish about it. If I was going to be fool enough to do somebody else's work — i.e., his — well then, so be it.

I could not resist him any longer. I knelt down beside him, took him in my arms and, ignoring how dirty he was, gave him a hug. I hugged so long that he let out a small and surprised-sounding "aeiou," but other than that, he did nothing. I'm sure it was the first hug, or sign of human affection, he had had for a very long time, if indeed ever in his life. After that, I began his bath and, without a sound or a hiss or a single pullback, he let me wash away to my heart's content — first gently and then, as I went through literally layers of dirt, harder and harder.

In good time, having made several trips to the bathroom to rinse out the cloths, I had scrubbed enough to make a startling discovery. Underneath all the dirt he was neither tan nor gray, the two colors which I had fully expected. He was, instead, white.

I could hardly contain my excitement — at which the now much cleaner tail for the first time in the operation, moved. "What color did you expect?" it was inquiring. "Purple?" Almost in spite of myself, I heard myself answer him. "But you were so *dirty*," I protested. "White was the last color I expected."

After I had him reasonably presentable, at least for a first effort, and had towelled him dry, I stood up and inspected him. His green eyes with his by now relatively clean and pure white face made him look, for the first time, beautiful. Indeed to me, at that moment, he looked so beautiful that I had an urge simply to stare. I knew that few animals liked to be stared at, and that when a human being did so, they usually looked away. But he did not look away. He looked steadily back at me. Once more I bent and hugged him.

When the doorbell rang again, it was, of course, Mrs. Wills. But when I ushered her into the living room to review the subject at hand, the subject was, once again, not at hand. He had repaired, as usual, to his prepared position.

I handed her the flashlight. By now Mrs. Wills had grown accustomed to getting down on her hands and knees as part of the inspection tour, and she gamely turned on the flashlight and pushed her head under the sofa. "My God," she exclaimed suddenly, "he's white." Her head turned to me suspiciously. "Are you sure," she demanded, "that this is the same cat?" I assured her that it was, and indicated the pile of washcloths and towels lying on the hearth as proof. "I can't believe it," she said.

"It was nothing," I shrugged. "Just a matter of know-how and stick-to-itiveness. But you were right, Mrs. Wills. White cats do take an awful lot of work."

Mrs. Wills paid no attention. Instead, she was entirely concerned with making contact under the sofa. "Here, kitty, kitty," she called. She called it again — in fact, she called everything but kitchy-koo. Naturally, nothing worked. Mrs. Wills reached. The cat moved. Mrs. Wills reached again. The cat moved again. This stylized duet went on for some moments. Then Mrs. Wills pulled herself up and went over and sat down in a chair. She chose one, I noticed, directly across from the sofa. I sat down beside her.

"I've never had an animal in my life react to me like that," she said. "I've never even met one who wouldn't meet me halfway. I've always had a way with animals."

I told her that was just the trouble; he thought that she was going to take him away. Mrs. Wills ignored my bad pun. "I've never," she said firmly, "seen any animal *that* shy."

Once, I offered, I had had a schoolmaster who told us there was no such thing as being shy. He said that being shy was just being conceited, that you thought everybody was looking at you and thinking about you and of course they weren't.

Mrs. Wills now looked at me as if I had two heads. But she was still clearly considering the cat. "He's so pretty," she said. "Jennifer would love him."

It was time to pull out all the stops. Of course, I said, it might not be just shyness — you really never could tell.

But on the other hand, it might be something else. I reminded her that white cats were, after all, albinos — and often deaf.

"Deaf!" she exclaimed. "You mean maybe he can't hear me calling?"

I told her that it was entirely possible — perhaps he could not.

For the first time Mrs. Wills looked doubtful. "I don't really know much about white cats," she said.

I moved in swiftly.

"It's not just the deafness," I told her; "it's the skin problems, too. White cats, you know, can have terrible skin trouble."

Now she looked positively uncomfortable. "Well," I went on relentlessly, "I'm sure it's not contagious. How old is Jennifer?"

"Ten," she replied worriedly.

"Well, I suppose she could wear gloves," I suggested. "Of course, skin problems can make a cat edgy. Fortunately, he isn't very large. But he certainly can be fierce. And he sure can swipe." I indicated the scratches on face and neck. "He really got me one awful one. Fortunately, he didn't get near my eyes. Does Jennifer wear glasses?"

Mrs. Wills' own eyes were now riveted on me. "It was nothing, of course," I said, "and Ruth Dwork was quick at staunching the blood." I paused. "Just the same, I don't think it would be wise, at least in the beginning, to leave Jennifer alone with him."

She looked back down at the bottom of the sofa. "But anyway," I went on, "he'll probably be at the vet most of the first several months anyway. You were so right about that crooked way he stands. He'll need at least one operation, for sure."

Mrs. Wills said nothing for a long while. Then a smile slowly started across her face. "Mr. Amory," she asked, "are you planning to keep this cat yourself?"

It was my turn to smile. "Why, Mrs. Wills," I said, "whatever gave you that idea?"

She got up and picked up the cat carrier. "A little bird told me," she said. I started to apologize for her trouble in having to come to the apartment twice. "Don't," she said. "And don't call Ruth Dwork. I want the fun of telling her how it all happened." She paused a last time. "I wish you all the luck in the world with your cat." She grinned and got in a last jab. "From what you've just told me about him," she said, "you're going to need it. Merry Christmas."

It was by now close to lunchtime and I had an engagement. When I went back to say good-bye to the cat, however, I was spared the under-the-sofa routine. He was once more in the middle of the living room. On the spur of the moment, there and then, I decided it was time to initiate our first real man-to-cat talk. I told him that I had been for some time a bachelor. And aside from having an occasional stray animal for a short period, I had lived alone. At the same time, I realized that he had lived in the — I put it as inoffensively as I could — well, wild and was thus used to fending for himself and in a sense living alone too. We were both used to making our own decisions. But now if we were going to live together in any degree of harmony, there would have to be compromises on both sides.

I, for example, would have to learn that he had his needs and I would have to learn to distinguish when he wanted company and when he wanted to be alone. And,

I continued, he would have to understand the same things about me. There could be and should be, I said, give-and-take on both sides in almost all matters. But in matters where there was disagreement and a resolution would have to be made, there could only be one person to make it. And that person would be me.

At this his tail, which had begun a slow movement, suddenly began to move faster. It was my first encounter with expecting agreement from him and getting instead not disagreement but something curiously in-between. He was obviously considering it all but by no means entirely going along with it. I had no idea what was going on in his mind but somehow it seemed to me that what I was saying was so complicated that it was something he would have to take up in committee. And his idea of committee was first to look away and then to yawn and finally to start washing himself. The signs were unmistakable. That while his committee might be in session — indeed while it might at that very moment be taking the matter under advisement — in no case was it about to be rushed into a hasty decision.

Suddenly it seemed to me essential for our future that I not allow myself to be bogged down by his kind of bureaucracy. Sternly I told him that he might as well understand now and for once and for all something else. That bachelors have a reputation for being — and I emphasized this strongly — Very Set In Their Ways.

This time the answer, together with the tail rat-tat, came instantly. So, he was replying, with exactly the same emphasis, Are Cats.

The conflict was begun — and the issue joined.

III ∘ *The Great Compromise*

Some years ago the distinguished English author Aldous Huxley wrote a brief essay which he began as follows:

> I met, not long ago, a young man who aspired to become a novelist. Knowing that I was in the profession, he asked me to tell him how he should set to work to realize his ambition. I did my best to explain. "The first thing," I said, "is to buy quite a lot of paper, a bottle of ink, and a pen. After that you merely have to write."
>
> But this was not enough for my young friend. He seemed to have a notion that there was some sort of esoteric cookery book, full of literary recipes, which you had only to follow attentively to become a Dickens, a Henry James, a Flaubert. . . .
>
> . . . Did I keep a notebook or a daily journal? Did

I systematically frequent the drawing rooms of the rich and fashionable? Or did I, on the contrary, inhabit the Sussex downs? Or spend my evenings looking for "copy" in East End gin-palaces? . . .

And so on. I did my best to reply to these questions — as non-committally, of course, as I could. And as the young man still looked rather disappointed, I volunteered a final piece of advice, gratuitously. "My young friend," I said, "if you want to be a psychological novelist and write about human beings, the best thing you can do is to keep a pair of cats." And with that I left him.

If I had read this essay before I had rescued my cat, I would probably have thought that Mr. Huxley had gone around the bend. By Christmas night with my new cat, however, I no longer thought so — specifically from the time, that very second night I had him, when, just before I had gone to sleep, he had suddenly jumped up on the bed, marched solemnly up to my head, and then stretched out by the back of my neck. After that, I was in no condition to make any judgments about Mr. Huxley. If he was around the bend, I was most assuredly all the way up the river.

And, when I had the chance, I eagerly devoured the rest of Mr. Huxley's essay — one which bore the intriguing title "Sermon in Cats." In it, Mr. Huxley went on to give the young man specific instructions. He was, for example, to procure the "tailed variety" of cat — indeed, the man was firmly warned against getting himself a pair of Manx cats and thus, presumably, making his study more difficult. "The tail in cats," Mr. Huxley declared, "is the principal organ of emotional expression." The author also counselled his student not only to watch his cats

"living from day to day" but also to do more than this —
"to mark, learn and inwardly digest the lessons about
human nature which they teach."

In any case, whether it was because, consciously or
unconsciously, I was following Mr. Huxley's advice, or
simply because I enjoyed what I was doing, the fact was
that, in the first days after I had rescued my cat, I spent
a great deal of time just looking at him. I even did so,
indeed I particularly did so, when he was sleeping. These
were the best times, I found, for wondering what his life
had been. All cats sleep an amazing amount — close to
three-quarters of the time, I would estimate, counting, of
course, the kind of nap which they have made famous.
But he slept those first days even more than three-quarters
of the time — clearly to compensate for the many hours
he must have had to stay awake and alert during his
previous life. I also presumed that he was sleeping more
now because he was now happy. I was already a firm
believer in the theory that one of the ways in which cats
show happiness is by sleeping.

During his sleep he was obviously some of the time
dreaming. In these dreams, he would twitch, often gently
but at other times violently, both front and back paws
moving — sometimes indeed so violently that he woke
himself. At such times, during these sudden wake-ups, he
would be alert very quickly. Then, after a brief look around
and a casing of all fronts, he would do a definite double-
take. Finally, after satisfying himself that the waking, not
the dream, the present, not the past, was the reality, he
would blow out a little sigh — he never really heaved
one — and immediately go back to sleep.

I have read a great deal about what animals dream, but

none of it has ever really satisfied me. I believe they dream exactly the way we dream, and about everything in their lives — that they have good dreams and bad dreams in almost direct proportion, as we do, to whether their lives have been more good than bad. Unfortunately, because the majority of animals have it so much tougher than we do, I believe that the majority of dreams, except in the most fortunate petdom, are bad.

Nor do I believe, as I have also read, that, because animals have shorter memories than we do, they do not remember things as well. In the first place, I do not think they have shorter memories than we do — I think they have, if anything, longer ones. And, in the second place, I think they remember their dreams just as well as we do, and perhaps even better. I, for example, am a terrible dream-rememberer. If I don't concentrate on what I've been dreaming the moment I wake up, it is a very rare dream indeed that gets remembered past breakfast. On the other hand, I can tell by the manner in which my cat assumes his thinker position — front paws under him, head looking straight ahead, but eyes half shut — that he can certainly remember his dreams long after breakfast. And the only reason he is not thinking about them before breakfast is that, at that time, he is just thinking about breakfast. His thought process is very orderly.

As to what he dreamed about in those early days, I can easily imagine. To begin with, I knew from his teeth and other indicators that he was about two years of age when I rescued him. I was also fairly certain, from his cuts and bruises, his paper-thinness and generally poor condition, that he had been on the street if not all his short life, at least for most of it. But how long had he led a solitary life, the way he was when I found him? Surely he must have some time before been with other cats, at least back when he himself was a kitten? Or had he been someone's pet and perhaps gotten out and gotten lost and become a stray? Or had he perhaps been abandoned deliberately and, in that awful phrase, "gotten rid of"? These were all questions to which I would never know the answer.

Of some things, on the other hand, I could be fairly certain. One was that he had never been in a pound. There are only two ways out for animals at pounds — being adopted or being killed. And cats have such a low rate of adoption that many pounds, even in some large cities, don't bother to take them in at all. Not for nothing is it always the "dog pound" and never the "cat pound." And even at the best shelters, the adoption rate for cats is sadly low.

On the street, as strays, it is true that cats have certain advantages over dogs. They are quicker and can get away from trouble faster. They are smarter about locating hide-aways, and, being smaller, can fit into them less visibly. They can also forage for food more adeptly and, when they find it, have far better sense about what will and will not make them sick.

But here the advantages end and the disadvantages begin. Cats are notably clean animals and are sensitive, even fastidious, about their surroundings. A life in dirt and noise and confusion is hard on them. And, in this street life, they have a far more difficult time defending themselves. Stray cats, like stray dogs, often band together for safety, but being more individually territorial, they are more inclined than dogs to fight among themselves. Also, unlike dogs, although they may hide together, they almost never run in packs or actually fight together against common enemies. And these enemies, after all, include for them not only all the enemies dogs have but, for them, the dogs as well.

Then too, although as many people like cats as like dogs, there are far more people who don't like cats than who don't like dogs. There is no one go-away word for dogs as there is for cats — that curious expletive "scat!" There is some prejudice against dogs among non-animal people, but the prejudice against cats runs much more deeply. Some children tie tin cans and firecrackers to dogs' tails, it is unhappily true, but they only go so far for fear of being bitten. A cornered cat, however, is not regarded as dangerous and is considered fair game. Even kittens are not immune from such sport. By no means the worst of their torments, albeit it is probably the most stupid, is being picked up and dropped from heights to see if they really do always land on their feet.

Besides the fact that he had been thrown at and hit with things and had been severely cut, what else, I kept wondering, had been done to him? I found myself thinking of a film I had seen many years ago about a day in the life of a stray cat. The film had been made by the Pasadena Humane Society, and I have always remembered one scene — shot at cat's-eye level. It was of the cat trying at night to cross a California freeway. He was looking for any possible way to get across all those lanes — in the midst of all the screaming noise, the blinding headlights, the whizzing cars, and the monster trucks.

The film made you wish that we all, at one time in our life, would have to get down — really lie down — to the eye level of a small animal and have to look at the world from that perspective, to see how huge everything is and how terrifying. I even allowed myself to think about how enormous I must have seemed to my cat on that very first night when I rose to my feet and stuffed him in my coat.

His attitude toward me in those first days was fascinating. He showed me over and over, not just by happy tail talk, but, even more definitely, by delicate brushing against my legs, that he was, and apparently always would be, extremely grateful that I had effected his rescue. But at the same time he showed me in various other ways — by disappearances and actual yowlings if I had left him alone for too long — that the gratitude he felt toward me should in no way be construed by me as having anything to do with what was, to him, becoming every day more painfully obvious — that I had an incredible amount to learn about the art of living with him in any sort of civilized manner.

As anyone who has ever been around a cat for any length of time well knows, cats have enormous patience with the limitations of the human mind. They realize that, whether they like it or not, they are simply going to have to put up with what to them are excruciatingly slow mental processes, that we humans have embarrassingly low I.Q.'s, and that probably because of these defects, we have an infuriating inability to understand, let alone follow, even the simplest and most explicit of directions.

As if this weren't enough for them to cope with, they must also deal with what, for them, is almost equally frustrating — our tremendous physical shortcomings. The fact is that, to cats, we humans are, for all our grotesque size, unbelievably slow and clumsy. We are totally incapable of managing a good leap or jump or pounce or swipe or, indeed, almost any other simple maneuver which, at the very least, would make us passable fun to play with. It is not difficult to see how they arrive at these conclusions. Any self-respecting cat can, for example, leap with ease, from a standing start, to the mantelpiece — a leap some seven times or more his height. And yet the human record for the high jump, for pity sakes, for which we get a running start, is barely twice our height. Furthermore, since cats see at eye level so much of where this puny power of ours comes from — our ankles — they are obviously not averse to comparing our ankles with their own dainty and tiny-tendoned back legs.

Carrying this thought a step further, is it not possible that cats equate our pathetic slowness afoot with our slowness amind? If we are so handicapped physically, in other words, how could we expect it not to affect us mentally? Whether it does or not, they seem to realize, early on, that their task of training us is not going to be an easy one and can only be accomplished with extraordinary resolution and dedication on their part. They sense that it is absolutely essential for them to seize every opportunity for education and correction. Otherwise, as befitting our slothful natures, we will slip back immediately into our most incorrigible old habits. Their job in this regard is something, I'm told, like a wife's. The fact that I have been repeatedly told it, as well as the fact that, as I have said, I am a fairly recent bachelor, is something on which I am much given to speculation.

Not to put too fine a point on the matter, the fact also is that, having always had dogs myself, I had long held the theory that, in general, men prefer dogs and women prefer cats. I had even, pre-cat, defended this position with what I had always considered unassailable logic — male, of course.

To begin with, I started with such a basic as the cat's use of the litter pan. To women, this was proof positive of the advantage of the feline over the canine — not to mention that it obviates the necessity of a walk in inclement weather and ruining their hair. To men, on the other hand, it was something one knew about cats, but hardly more than that. Indeed, I had taken it for granted that my cat would, as he did, use his litter pan the very first night I had him. I did not even consider that the makeshift version, filled with torn-up newspaper, which Marian and I had contrived, may well have been the first one he had ever seen.

Besides this there is, for women, the added lure of the ability of the cat — something which is totally beyond the powers of the dog — not only to be able to clean himself, but also to want to do so and, in fact, do so repeatedly. To women, many of whom I have known who prefer a bath to any other engagement they can think of, and, indeed, give it precedence over any other — this appeal is irresistible.

But integral as were all these points to my theory, they were still relatively minor surface issues. The cutting edge of my theory and the crux of my logic involved something far more important. This was that the main reason women preferred cats over dogs was that they identified with, and much more strongly than men appreciated, the cat's independence. And that they did this because, up until fairly recently, at least, they had so little of it themselves.

Men, on the other hand, not only did not appreciate the cat's independence, they thoroughly detested it. Indeed, they immeasurably preferred the image of the devoted dog curled at their feet, the faithful companion who would obey without question his master's slightest whim, who would accompany him anywhere — at a walk, a jog, or even a run — and who would, above all, come when he was called no matter what he was doing, even if he were chasing a cat.

The fact that the cat, in contrast, would not even acknowledge the simplest command, let alone deign to obey it, and would seldom, if ever, come when called, even if doing nothing else — all this to men was not only disturbing, it also could mean only one of two things. Either the cat did not love them or, worse, the cat was part and parcel of the kind of revolution which, in the end, would result not only in anarchy in the street but right in their home and hearth.

I had, as I say, long held this theory. But, all of about twenty-four hours after I had had my cat, I was suddenly not so sure. And, if there's one thing I do not like to be, it is to be made suddenly less sure of something which, only a matter of hours before, I have been absolutely sure. In any case, I decided that I owed it to my cat to make a clean breast of it — at least to let him know, pre-him, where I was coming from.

Curiously, at about the same time as I made that decision, my cat, already constantly on the alert for opportunities to educate and, if need be, correct me, was coming to a decision of his own. We were on collision course.

The matter came to a head the day after Christmas. It came about, as a matter of fact, because of a present Marian had brought back to him on Christmas night — a yarn ball which she had brought over from the pile of presents given to our office cats. Although he had undoubtedly played with many things in his young life, I could tell right away from the way he went at that ball that he had never had a real toy before.

All that evening he batted it and bit it and tossed it and squashed it — and, of course, lost it. And, after he had done this, it was clearly up to me to get it back for him, even though I had the feeling he knew perfectly well where it was and even when this place was somewhere under the sofa, from which he could have retrieved it far more easily than I.

It was on approximately my eighth service as golden retriever that I conceived the first of my masterly notions on how to train him. I had once read an article by a man who had apparently trained many cats and remembered that the man had counselled, among other things, that with cats, in preference to the dog commands of "Sit," "Lie Down," and "Play Dead," the roommate of a cat should use "Sit," "Flop," and "Sleep." And also that, even with these changes, it was sometimes necessary to give what the man suggested was a "slight touch." Armed with this information and also with the determination to turn our play period into not just play but into a learning experience — something which gave me the good feeling that I was in the forefront of modern educational theory — this time, when I brought the ball back, instead of throwing it to him I threw it a little way from him. "Go get it," I told him earnestly. "Fetch." To which I not only added the masterly "slight touch," which in this case was a slight push, but also at the same time patted my leg. My meaning was crystal clear. He was to go and get the ball and bring it back to me.

His answer to this plan — one which was designed both to con him into being the one to do the retrieving and at at the same time to establish a clearly defined chain of command — was disconcerting. Instead of, for a single moment, entertaining the slightest idea of actually doing what I wanted, he had obviously and instantly decided to turn my whole master plan into a learning experience, all right — but one, equally obviously, not for him but for me.

First he sat down and looked at the ball and then sternly at me. He thumped his tail slowly, not once but twice. Cats, he was patiently but firmly trying to get into my head, do not fetch, or retrieve, or do any of those other unbelievably undignified things which might, in fact, be done by other animals whose name he obviously preferred not to mention in the present company.

I must have looked completely taken aback because, as he kept his green eyes fixed on me, his tail tone seemed to gentle just a little. And, he went on, in what was nonetheless a more patient manner, it was up to me to understand that it was not that cats did not like games. They did indeed enjoy games and as a matter of fact put more into their games and got more out of them than any of those selfsame animals he had declined to mention before. However, these games must be games that *they* wanted to play, and must be games initiated by them — after which, of course, if the pace of action could be improved or perhaps speeded up by the enlistment of outsiders (here he clearly meant me and my ability to get down on my knees and reach under things) — well, that, of course, could be considered. But it could only be considered on that basis, and in that order and never — and here the tail beat a final rat-tat — the other way around.

Obviously, it was time for another of our man-to-cat talks. "Come here," I told him. "Come," I repeated, lest there be any mistake.

This time he looked at me as if it was not possible for him to have heard what he thought he had heard. Even allowing for my obviously brief attention span, to have talked about fetching and retrieving and then, almost in the next breath, to have uttered this "Come" — it was really much too much. He was clearly working with a person who, in the words of the wise old saw, was not playing with a full deck. He was a tolerant cat, and he would do what he could to improve my behavior patterns. And, just to avoid any possibility of misunderstanding, he would ask me one more time what I had said. But that, his tail warned, would be that.

I told him that it was indeed what I had said. And, I went on, as far as I was concerned, the only question now before the house was — would he do it?

Cats do not shake their heads. They do not need to. They do, however, shake their tails, and this he did, with what I can only describe as finality. Cats, he was clearly saying, do not come when called. Aha, I said. *Never?* What about when it was something they wanted — like dinner?

He visibly sighed. That, he was trying to explain to me, was an entirely different matter. And, as usual, I was bringing up a total irrelevance. If there was going to be any purpose whatsoever in our discussion, would I please stay on track?

It was my turn to sigh. Without for a moment conceding that dinner had nothing to do with the case, could he forget that for a moment and simply answer one single question. Why would he not come?

This time his answer could not have been clearer if he had said it in words. It was, he implied, the principle of the thing.

This was, to me, the final straw. Principle my foot, I said, knowing full well that he is not particularly fond of feet. I told him I had known many cats in my life, and, whether he liked it or not — indeed, whether he liked them or not — I had also known a very great many of that other animal which he did not care to name. And, I concluded firmly, the kind of animal I liked best was the kind to whom, when you said a simple thing like come — well, came.

To this he said nothing for some time. Indeed, it was such a length of time that I seriously considered that I had done permanent damage to our relationship or, much more probably, he was simply mulling over the horror of a person like myself having had to spend such a large segment of my life in the company of what he clearly regarded as a lesser species. In any case, I was soon faced with the end of our discussion, and what amounted to an ultimatum. Gracefully and lazily, he rose, walked past the ball, and settled down again on the far side of the room. Cats, he said, as distinctly as I ever heard him say anything, Do Not Come.

It was my turn to be patient. All right, I told him. It seemed to me that we were, once more, in an area of compromise. After all, if, through no real fault of my own, I had happened to have spent a large portion of my time with a subspecies which had resulted in my developing certain mind-sets and attitudes, and if, as a result of those said mind-sets and attitudes I was more comfortable with a friend who, when I said, "Come," well, came, wouldn't it be possible for him to realize the stress it visited on me to have to change those mind-sets and attitudes virtually overnight? And wouldn't it be possible for him, with that recognition, to make an occasional concession to my limited mental state and when I said, "Come" to — well, once again . . .

He yawned and started to take a bath. Obviously, our discussion was at an end, and the matter had gone to committee. Equally obviously, a decision would not be immediately forthcoming. Indeed, from the lack of vigor with which he was pursuing his bath, the committee was undoubtedly going to be in session all night.

As things turned out, I never did get a clear-cut decision. I did, however, come away with a compromise.

The way we worked it out was that I was never to say, "Come" or "Come here" or anything like that. Along with this, I was never, when I wanted him to come, to do anything to offend his sensibilities, such as slapping my knee, clapping my hands, whistling, or making clucking noises with my teeth. However, I would be permitted more subtle indications that his presence was requested — such as directing an inquiry to the world at large, or asking the room in general, where he was.

For his part, he agreed when he heard such general inquiries, not totally to ignore them. On the contrary, after a suitable period of time had elapsed — one long enough so that it could be clearly construed to be a moot point as to whether it was his decision or mine — he would, in a dignified and orderly manner, proceed in my direction.

In this way, and to the world at large, it would be clear that he had not failed his hallowed ancestors, who had fought so long and so gloriously the sacred fight for independence. He had not abdicated his responsibilities and he had not turned in either his badge or his union card as a cat. Nor had he defected, or become a mole. All he had done, in the interests of the pursuit of happiness, to insure domestic tranquility and to preserve a more perfect union for both of us, was to allow this previously seriously disadvantaged person to consider a small part of him — a very, very small part, to be sure — to be something like the animal which he did not care to dignify by mentioning by name. But it was to be completely understood, and indeed an integral part of our agreement, that the matter was now to be considered settled, for once and for all, and was never to be brought up for discussion again.

IV ○ *His First Trip*

In my Society writing days I once wrote a story about the late Mrs. E. T. Stotesbury, premier hostess of Palm Beach, who one day went to meet her husband, who had been on an extended European vacation. Mrs. Stotesbury had used the time he was away to have extensive work done on their Palm Beach castle, and she had somehow neglected to inform Mr. Stotesbury of the magnitude of this. But it was now obviously necessary to do so, and thus, just before entering the driveway, she broke, in her own way, the news.

"E. T.," she said, turning to her husband, "I have a surprise for you." Warily, Mr. Stotesbury turned and looked at his wife.

"Eva," he said, "husbands do not like surprises."

Somehow that story reminded me of my cat. For, in

this respect, cats are more like husbands than wives. They too do not like surprises.

Cats do, however, like routine — in fact they love it. And, in the days — and nights — which followed the rescue my cat and I worked out many routines. Or rather he worked them out, and I, as dutifully as I could, worked at following them.

Some of these routines necessarily involved compromises. My cat, for example, liked to get up early — in fact he liked to get up at 3 A.M. That was, of course, all right with me. His hours, it had been one of our understandings, were his own. The trouble was that, at 3 A.M., he liked a midnight snack of Tender Vittles. Again, seemingly, no problem. Simply leave out a bowl of Vittles before he went to bed.

But unfortunately there was a problem. I could not just leave out a bowl of Vittles before I went to bed. He would eat them before he went to bed. He did not have, when you came right down to it, either any good old-fashioned Boston discipline — as I would have thought he would have at least begun to learn from me — or, for that matter, my good sound sensible Boston foresight. No matter how large a bowl I filled of Vittles before he retired, the bowl was empty before he retired.

His hours in this routine thus became my hours. And so we compromised. Before going to bed each night, I put out an empty dish on the floor by the bed and a package of Tender Vittles on my bedside table. At 3 A.M. — and he was extraordinarily accurate about this — he would wake up, roll over, and wake me up. At 3:01 I would roll over, put some Vittles in his dish, or at least reasonably near it, and go back, or at least attempt to go back, to sleep.

In the real morning we had to have another compromise. This one was about water. Actually it is a fallacy to think all cats hate water. As a matter of fact, most large cats love water. A British friend of mine, John Aspinall, who has a privately owned animal park near Canterbury, had, in this park, both tigers and also a swimming pool. The tigers on hot days regularly took dips in the pool and often, when they wanted more company, would come up to John's front door, scratch, and give a tiger's version of a miaow — after which John would hastily don his swimming trunks, open the door, and then they would all make a beeline for the pool. Normally the tigers just went into the water any old way, but as time went on and they observed John diving off the board, they too would get up on the board and do their version of John's swan dive.

Small cats too are not averse to water, at least on hot days. Another friend of mine, Marti Scholl, a former New York model who had a television show in Las Vegas, used to take her two cats out with her to her swimming pool. One particularly hot day, after she had taken a dip, she detected what she thought was unusual interest in the proceedings from her cats. Without further ado, she took one cat under each arm and walked from the steps end of the pool out to where they were just above the water. Then, little by little, just as you would teach a child to swim, keeping one hand under them at first, she placed them in the water. In no time at all they were swimming away from her, back and forth to their hearts' content. Indeed, after just a couple of lessons, they were soloing — swimming the whole length of the pool up and back.

My cat was by no means as into this scene as were the cats of Mr. Aspinall or Ms. Scholl. At the same time, neither did he actively dislike all water. He just disliked vertical water — as in rain or shower baths. He did not mind it coming down in small quantities as out of a faucet — in fact he was very fond of it that way. But it had to be small quantities. If it was to be in large quantities, then he firmly insisted on his water being horizontal. This he was especially fond of when I was in it — as in a regular tub bath. He did not like the shower at any time, whether I was in it or not.

So, again, we compromised. Although I had always taken showers, I gave up showers and took tubs instead. Baths, I decided, really get you much cleaner than showers do anyway. Also, whether this was true or not, I very much liked the additional routine which he had developed, and which I had followed, which went with the bath. What he would do, once I was in the tub, was to jump up on the edge of the tub — a precarious leap, considering his game hip — balance himself, and then make a slow solemn trip around. He would start first toward the back of the tub, stopping at each point when he got to my shoulders. Here he would lean toward me, give me a head nudge and a small nip, and then proceed on. When he got to the business end of the tub, he would carefully investigate the spout, and, if I had not turned it on just enough for him to drink a few drops, he would turn and tell me to do so. And, of course, I would.

I enjoyed our bath routine as much as any we did. One day, however, I read an article in, I think, *Cat Fancy* magazine, in which a woman wrote that one of the most charming things her cat did was to take a bath with her. She then proceeded to tell the story of her baths with her cat and tell it almost exactly as I have — even including the nudge and nip of the shoulder and neck and also the investigation of, and drinking from, the spout.

At first, thinking my cat and my cat only had ever done such a wonderful thing, I was extremely annoyed by the article. Nonetheless, on second thought, I consoled myself by thinking that if there were only two cats in the world who ever did it, my cat and that writer's cat, then it wasn't really too bad. And, after all, that writer had at least thought it was remarkable enough to write an article about it.

I still did have, however, a gnawing doubt — enough so that one day I approached a cat friend of mine and asked her right out if she had ever taken a bath with her cat. "Oh, yes," she at once replied, "and you know, when we're taking a bath together, he does the cutest thing. He jumps . . ."

I know, I said, sternly stopping her, so does mine. There were now, I thought, not just two but three, and how many others? Perhaps, I harbored the sneaking suspicion, there were hundreds of thousands of cats out there who all did it, and had been doing it for hundreds of years or at least ever since bathtubs were invented. For all I knew it had gone out over the cat grapevine that, if you do the bath thing, humans are so dumb they will think you're the only cat who does it. Perhaps the grapevine might even have added that even if humans don't think you're the only one who does it, and you do it in the morning, it's bound to put them in such a good mood that at the very least you'll be assured a bigger and better breakfast.

It was, I decided, not something on which I wished to dwell. Speaking of breakfast, however, I want to make clear that my cat and I did not have, by any stretch of the imagination, your normal morning repast. Indeed, perhaps the most remarkable of all the routines which we developed was here involved. For the plain fact of the matter is that, before its development anywhere else, and long before its adoption by the upper echelons of big business, my cat and I pioneered, all by ourselves, the power breakfast.

This too began with a compromise. My cat was very fond of breakfast, and, after he had eaten his, he was very fond of eating mine too. In vain I remonstrated with him that he was being selfish and inconsiderate. In vain also I lectured him that I had been brought up in a home where animals were not allowed in the dining room at any time, even when no meals were being served. As for his habit, without so much as a by my leave, of getting up on the table and taking a bite here and a bite there, of anything he pleased, from cereal to eggs or whatever, it would have to stop. It simply could not or would not be tolerated by me, and that was that.

So, once more, we compromised. I agreed to let him up on the table if no other guests were present, and he in turn agreed not to eat anything at the same time I was eating it. The gray area in this compromise was the question of when I had my spoon or fork in my mouth, and he was not sure whether or not it was going back to where it came from or was finished: whose turn, then, was it — his or mine? Eventually we worked this out — if the spoon was still in motion, it was still my turn; if it wasn't, it was his.

All in all, it was a power breakfast all right, and a great deal was accomplished. For one thing, when I was late and/or he was particularly hungry, I am sure we several times broke the standing Guinness record, and possibly the Olympic as well, for a single breakfast totally consumed by two partners.

It was, as a matter of fact, at one of these power breakfasts, when I got well ahead of him, that I noticed, for the first time close up, that his hip was still not well. The cut on his mouth had healed nicely, and his hip was some better, but it was by no means perfect. It was, in other words, high time that I took him to the vet. I had purposely put this off as long as I could — I did not want his settling in to be interrupted by the trauma of having to put him in a carrier and take him off to what I was sure he would think was away for good. But now the putting off could go on no longer. The hip was only part of the reason. He needed to be checked over, he needed an inoculation, and — worst of all — he would have to be neutered. Whether he did not go out or not, and whether or not he had any association with other cats, I, who had preached neutering and spaying for years, could simply not have a cat of my own which was not so "fixed."

Besides all this he was vigorously shaking his head a good deal. At first I thought it was just at some of my ideas, but, as it went on, even when I had not imparted any particular piece of advice, I realized that he was actually having trouble with his ears. This was not surprising. As I had told Mrs. Wills that first day, most white cats do. But it was again reason for taking him to the vet.

Another reason I had put off taking him to the vet was perhaps a subconscious one. In those days — and it was, after all, less than ten years ago — few veterinarians were at least publicly in sympathy with animal activists, or, as we were then called, "humaniacs." Although the veterinarian, like the doctors' famed Hippocratic Oath, took his oath too — "to use my scientific knowledge and skills for the relief of animal suffering . . . ," etc. — to the animal activist this oath, at least judging by the veterinarians' attitude toward us, seemed less Hippocratic than hypocritical. And some veterinarians, in turn, returned the favor. Indeed, some of the most vehement criticism I personally had taken came direct from their headquarters — from the American Veterinary Medical Association. I do not mean that I did not have vets as friends, or that some vets did not side publicly with me in some of my fights — I did and they did. But it does mean that these vets were the exception, not the rule.

To people outside the animal field, this might seem incredible. They read books about, and by, kindly vets who go around, at all hours of the day and night, doctoring animals and dispensing words which exude their love for them, they see animal movies and television shows in which the vet is the hero up against seemingly hopeless odds — albeit never against hunters or laboratories — and they may even have a child who loves animals very much and, when he or she grows up, wants nothing more than to be a vet and help animals. They are certain that all these kindly vets work hand in glove and on almost a daily basis with animal people and animal societies.

These same people outside of the animal field would sometimes drive into a city with which they were not familiar and, seeing more than once, the sign "Animal Hospital" — in fact thinking they saw more of these signs than for other hospitals — would immediately conclude they were in a very animal-oriented city, and would say something like, "This place seems to care more about sick animals than it does about sick people." Unfortunately, few of such people ever had the experience of picking up a sick or wounded animal by a roadside in or outside of such a town and then taking it to one of those "Animal Hospitals." If they had, they would often find that the "kindly" vet who ran the place would refuse to take the animal unless they met two conditions — first that they pretended it was their animal, not a stray, and second that they produced, in cash, at least fifty dollars.

One area in which the animal activist and the doctrinaire veterinarian of yesterday have long crossed swords is the matter of low-cost spay and neuter programs. While such efforts are surely an important attempt to do something about the cruel stray overpopulation problem, all too often in those days the veterinarians fought them tooth and nail. Such programs meant quite simply a loss of revenue, and, besides, they took the position that if they didn't keep spays and neuters, like their other services, at a uniform level, then well-off people who could afford to pay the regular price would simply take advantage of the lower fee, which was supposedly meant for poor people.

In fairness, there was some truth in this — an accurate gauge of who should pay the regular price and who the reduced was difficult to come by. But the net result of this opposition was that too often only humanely inclined veterinarians took part in such programs, and this in turn meant that these vets were intolerably overburdened. Today, with the success of such programs as Los Angeles' "Have A Heart," as well as the fact that more and more shelters are insisting that all pets be spayed or neutered before adoption, or at least as soon as possible thereafter, the situation is improving. And by no means the least of the reasons for this is the change in the mind-set of the veterinarian profession, particularly among its younger members. Where once vets had enjoyed a good laugh at the appearance, as far back as 1968, of the Fund for Animals' button "Animals Have Rights, Too," there is today a full-fledged and highly respected society called the Association of Veterinarians for Animal Rights.

Today indeed there is even reason for the same kind of optimism in the venerable struggle between activist and vet in the largest and most emotionally highly charged field of all — that of laboratory experimentation. A few years ago it was no easy task to get a veterinarian on "our side" who was willing to testify at a hearing in Washington or even in a state capital — the "other side," on the other hand, always seemed to have an endless supply of them. Nowadays, it's still not even-Steven, but we're gaining and this turnabout is, in at least this writer's opinion, long past high time. And for no animal more so than for the cat — the animal which, as any veterinarian should know, probably suffers more in the laboratory, because of his intense sensitivity, than any other.

There is, to begin with for the cat, the matter of his inherent cleanliness. In the early days, when the Fund for Animals was just beginning, I saw in laboratory after laboratory cage after cage which was just wire. It apparently made them easier to clean. And, for the people, I suppose it did. But for the cats, who had no way to stand except balanced on these thin wires and no way to sit or lie in any comfort at all, it was unbelievably heartless. On top of everything else — literally so in this — since there were cages above and below — urine and feces passed down through the cages on top of the cats below. No one apparently had considered litter boxes — indeed, most laboratories today still do not have them.

But the matter of his physical discomfort in the laboratory is, for the cat, just the beginning of his misery there. For this animal has the terrible bad luck of having a brain which, for all its small size, is not only, save for the ape, the most highly developed on the evolutionary scale, it is also the one most like the human brain. Actually, indeed, the cat's brain is so like ours that the only real difference the scientists have been able to find are in the memory association areas and the speech centers.

It is hardly surprising, then, that this remarkable little brain has, literally for centuries, been pried into by man. In the days before anesthesia the animals' agony must have been beyond imagination, but even today, when you see in virtually every major laboratory in the world hundreds of cats undergoing hundreds of brain experiments — all with the telltale electrodes firmly implanted not onto but into their little heads — it is an unnerving and indeed heartrending sight.

And, speaking of nerves, the cat has another and equally terrible piece of bad luck — his whole nervous system. Indeed, if his brain is so close to ours as to give us, in more ways than one, pause, his nervous system is so close as to be almost eerie. And so, of course, for the cat and the cat alone are reserved the most horrendous psychological experiments the mind of man can conjure up — and be paid for. So widespread, in fact, is this kind of experimentation that it is not by any means limited to bona fide laboratories. A twenty-year experiment, for example, involving millions of dollars of research grants, was recently spent to study, of all subjects, the effects of mutilation of tomcats on their sex life. The locale of the study was, of all places, at the American Museum of Natural History in New York, where, among other things, the experimenters blinded cats, deafened cats, and destroyed the cats' sense of smell, not to mention removing parts of their brains and their sexual organs.

Although these experiments were eventually stopped, they were not stopped because the museum itself disowned them — they were stopped because, as the president of the museum himself informed me, they had lost one-third of their membership over them.

Although few cruelties in the animal field any longer surprise me, the psychological experiments on cats still do. Two of them particularly stand out in my mind. One took place at Stanford University, where a Dr. William Dement achieved a certain stardom among his colleagues by establishing what I believe is still the standing world record for keeping a cat deprived of sleep. Dr. Dement kept one cat so deprived, on a brick surrounded by water, for seventy days.

The other experiment took place at the other end of the country, at the Veterans Hospital in Northport, Long Island. Here the researcher had at his disposal a wide variety of mother cats and their kittens. His procedure was to separate the mother cat from her kitten and then, when the kitten approached the mother, to give it electrical shocks through a device attached to its leg. These shocks increased in intensity as the kitten approached its mother, and the researcher began giving the shocks seven days after the births of the kittens and continued doing it for thirty-five days, right through the nursing period.

During this time he became, he wrote, interested in the behavior of the mother cats, although, he said, they were not part of the experiment. These mothers would, he noted, do everything possible to "thwart," as he put it, the experiment. They both bit and used their claws. They also tried to bite the electrode wires. And they of course tried to run over and comfort their kittens. But when this only got the kittens even more severe shocks, the mothers eventually pulled away and even tried to keep the kittens from them by striking at them.

The researcher was obviously fascinated by all this, and

all the time he was studying, his paper made clear, juvenile delinquency — the same subject, incidentally, which the Museum of Natural History was supposedly studying with the tomcats.

The veterinarian I chose for my cat was one who I knew felt as I did about such outrages. Her name was Susan Thompson and, among other distinctions, she had, twenty years before, been the only woman in her class at vet school. Before entering private practice, she had been on the staff of a shelter in which I was on the board, and I knew she was both extraordinarily professional and also had a rare combination of firmness and gentleness, and yet had the quickness that made it possible for her to do something which might be momentarily painful for the animal but was usually all over and the animal being petted before he knew what had happened. That, with a cat, is no mean achievement.

I called her and informed her of the high honor for which she had been nominated. She told me to bring the cat in the next morning and then listened to my diagnosis, as well as to my recital of all the virtues of my cat, with polite but I felt increasingly flagging interest until I got to the matter of his being "fixed." "If we're going to neuter," she interrupted, "I'll have to keep him overnight and I don't want you to give him anything to eat or drink after six o'clock tonight."

I knew she would have to keep him overnight, but I had not figured on the other matter. It was bad enough that I had to take him for the first time out of the apartment and entirely discombobulate him — just when he had become so settled and secure and happy — but that I also had to add to this putting him on a no-water, no-food regimen for all evening, all night, and even no power breakfast before his ordeal — well, it seemed doubly grim.

Nonetheless, there was nothing for it but to do it. And so all that evening, while he fussed for food, I did my best to distract him by telling him it wasn't my idea, it was other people's. I also did my best to distract him by extra fussing over him — by petting and playing. I even tried to get him to finish a baseball game we had developed with a Ping-Pong ball and which had ended in a dispute over a hit which he claimed was a home run and I claimed was a foul bunt. Unfortunately we had no instant replay available, and so my job was to get him to agree to actual replay. But over and over he would "aeiou" away, put out his paw, grab my leg, and attempt to move me toward the kitchen. When I refused he resorted to the most piteous "aeiou" I had ever heard. And, when bedtime came, he refused to get up on the bed.

At last, late that night, he finally gave up, jumped up on the bed and, not by my neck as he usually did but far down by my feet, lay down with an exaggerated and exasperated thump. At 3 o'clock, as usual, he awakened me, but when, even then, I made no move to deliver the Vittles, though he could clearly see the box and in fact had his eyes fixed on it, he had reached his breaking point. Obviously I had lost my mind, and from now on he would have to take matters into his own paws. With one agile leap, he was over me and on the bedside table, with one swift cuff he had the box overturned, and then, just when he was about to settle in, I made my move. I too swooped over and up and grabbed.

He looked at me with a look that said we have met the enemy and it is you, but I ignored it. Instead, I put the Vittles back in the box and the box in a drawer. As for him, he turned his back, jumped to the floor and, for the rest of the night, stayed there.

The next morning I settled the matter of the power breakfast with, if I do say so, a bold and masterful maneuver. I decided I would not, that morning, have breakfast either. No one, after all, needs breakfast every morning.

I went instead to the closet and brought down a carrier — one which Marian, with her usual foresight, had surreptitiously brought in and placed, out of his sight, on an upper shelf. The trouble was that the moment I took it out, although I was sure he had never seen a carrier before, the jig was up. He somehow knew something was going on about which he was highly suspicious, and that whatever this something was, it had to do with whatever that stupid thing — i.e., the carrier — was. Immediately it became apparent to me that not only did he not have the slightest intention of getting into the thing, he would not come anywhere near it.

As I was pondering how to handle this situation, I remembered reading somewhere that, before you tried to get your cat into a carrier, you should be sure he is both properly introduced to it and also has a chance to make friends with it — that he should be given the opportunity to play around it and even in it, by putting one of his toys in it — and that all this should be done well before you even think of taking him somewhere in it.

Of course I had not done this, and now it was too late. I also remembered the experience of a friend of mine, Pia Lindstrom, of television fame. Ms. Lindstrom at that time had two cats, and, she told me, she made her first trip to her vet with one cat in her carrier and the other cat under her arm. The first cat, she said, didn't mind the carrier at all, the second did. He would not be enticed in, and he would not — even with two people, one to hold him and the other to hold the carrier — be forced in. Thus she went to the vet as she went everywhere else — with one cat in and one cat out.

When she arrived, the vet assumed that either her cats didn't get along or that she thought two were too many in one carrier, or perhaps she was just a typically careless celebrity. In any case, he was all help. "Here," he said, "I'll take that one — I have another carrier in the other room." Ms. Lindstrom pulled away. "Oh no," she said, "don't bother. He won't get in." The vet demanded to know what she meant. Ms. Lindstrom repeated what she meant. But the vet wouldn't hear of it. "Nonsense," he said. And, with that, he seized her cat and started for the other room — and the carrier.

Ms. Lindstrom watched them disappear and heard the door shut. That was not, however, the last thing she heard. For what she next heard, she reported objectively, as she was trained to do, was the outbreak of World War III. She heard what sounded like chairs being overturned, possibly even tables, and various things landing on the floor. She also heard unmistakable human swearwords alternated with equally unmistakable cat yowls. And finally she heard total silence.

In a moment the vet, carrying his carrier, appeared. His shirt was ripped and there was blood on his arms. The carrier was fine, but, inside, there was no cat. Finally, like a streak of lightning, her cat went by the vet and leapt into her lap.

The vet put down the carrier, but at a respectable distance from both Ms. Lindstrom and the cat. "I don't think," he said, still panting, "he likes carriers." "No," said Ms. Lindstrom, trying not, at that particular moment, to pat her cat, "he doesn't."

After I finished thinking about that story, I started thinking about the task at hand — getting my cat into the carrier. I was, of course, determined not to use brute force, and so, after studying him for a moment, I decided to make a game of it. First I put the carrier as close to him as I dared, got down on my hands and knees, opened it, and showed him how terrific it was — how you could even see from inside it. To illustrate this I put my face right in it and looked out at him from under the isinglass cover. I even thought of pretending to eat something in there. I decided, however, that, under the circumstances of his enforced fast, this would be too cruel, and so, instead, I concentrated on attempting to show him how interesting it was in there — particularly with the nice soft blanket underneath and everything. He, however, evinced not the slightest interest in my interest and, in any case, whatever interest he did have he was determined to take my word for. One thing he would not do was come one step closer to it.

I looked at my watch — there was no more time. With one swooping motion with my hand I reached out, scooped him up, and put him, almost before he knew what was happening, inside. At the same time, with the other hand, I closed the cover and locked it.

He looked at me from inside with a look which, woebegone as it was, nonetheless clearly asked at least three questions. Was it not enough that I had tried to deceive him? Did I also have to resort to that typical human reaction of using total force? And finally, did I, after the ultimate betrayal, have, beyond it, a still darker plan?

I refused to answer any of the questions. Instead, I bravely looked away. I put on my coat, picked up the carrier, strode to the door, opened it, and marched to the elevator. The worst of it all — the ride in the elevator, the walk to the garage, the wait for the car and then putting him in — was that I was sure he felt he was now going to be put back where he had come from. To counteract this, when we were on our way in the automobile and he was in the seat beside me, I opened the top of the carrier and put my arm on top of him. I wanted him to be able to see that at least we were not going where he had been before, but at the same time I had not the slightest desire of letting him out of the carrier and investigating the scenery better. I was sure I could never get him back in.

Fortunately I found, near Dr. Thompson's office, a pretty good place, at least by New York standards, to park. A ticket, in other words, wasn't an absolutely sure thing.

One interesting thing about Dr. Thompson's office is that, while you have a day appointment, you do not have a time appointment. That is run on a strictly first-come, first-served basis — except, of course, in case of emergency. The other, and more interesting, thing is that in Dr. Thompson's office there is not an office manager. Or rather, there is an office manager, but it is not a person. It is a cat.

The cat's name is Blacky. Blacky came to Dr. Thompson from an owner who was tired of Blacky being sick and, though he was not old, decided to have him, in that euphemism, "put down." Dr. Thompson, however, decided otherwise, and, after reaching an agreement with the owner, kept Blacky.

Almost at once Blacky took over the office and has

remained as manager ever since. He was literally "on the desk" as I walked in. I immediately went up to him and explained my business. He listened attentively, and, I could have sworn, checked his list. Anyway, whether he did or not, when I put down the carrier, Blacky rose up and solemnly peered down at my cat. My cat equally solemnly peered back. Even through the isinglass there was, I could see, immediate rapport.

It was a good start, and since Blacky all but indicated where I was to sit, I went over and sat there. In the circle of seats there were two cats, one small dog, and one enormous Great Dane — all with their people. Blacky had indicated a seat in the cat section, the farthest distance from the Dane, but the woman who owned the Dane was, unfortunately, the most interested in me. She was complimentary about my animal work, but the more interested she became in telling me about this, the less she controlled her dog. And, since I had once more opened the top of the carrier, the next thing I knew he was eyeball to eyeball with the Dane. "AEIOU," he hissed, just as I put my hand between him and an animal for which he would make, at best, an hors d'oeuvre. Fortunately the woman at that moment got ahold of her dog, but she was now by no means as enchanted with me. "Surely you of all people," she said sternly, pulling her dog away, "should know that Danes are the gentlest of all big dogs."

Surely I did, I told her, but somehow I had neglected to inform my cat of that fact.

The rest of that wait was by no means my favorite — and I am not a good waiter under the best of circumstances. One of the cat women was the next to take an interest in me — or rather my cat. "And what is our name?" she asked, sticking her fingers in at him. I told her he didn't have a name yet — what with Christmas and all. She looked at me as if I were some distance from her concept of a fit owner. "Oh dear," she said.

After what seemed an eternity — when all of the previous arrivals had been attended to, and a new group assembled — I was at last called. As if on cue, as I carried my cat in to Dr. Thompson, Blacky got up and walked with us. I had not believed Dr. Thompson when she told me that Blacky actually went in with new patients — but now I did believe it. And, when I took the cat out of the carrier and put him on her examining table, I noticed that Blacky had jumped up on one of the stools and was looking at him almost as intently as Dr. Thompson.

"Oh, he's a beauty," Dr. Thompson said — as I was sure she told all owners. But I noticed that as she ran her fingers over him, he did not tremble.

Once more I blurted out my diagnosis — of the mouth and the hip and the ears. Dr. Thompson is very used to patients' diagnoses, and she paid polite interest — but she did not stop her examination. She said nothing for some time, then gave it to me all at once. "The mouth is almost well," she said, "and the hip is coming along fine. I'm going to let it heal its own way. I want to clean out his ears, though, but we can do that when we do the shots and the other thing. I also think we've got a little skin problem. He's got some allergies, but we'll do that another time."

I was almost glad he had some allergies. So many doctors, at the first sign of their patients having allergies, immediately prescribe the eviction of their cats. I felt it was nice cats could have some allergies of their own. Maybe, I suggested to Dr. Thompson, to doctors.

Dr. Thompson smiled. "Well," she said, "I'm going to

put him in the other room for a while until I finish with my other patients."

I was instantly all suspicion. Where? I wanted to know. Dr. Thompson showed me. "In here," she said, as she picked him up and I followed her into that other room. There were a lot of cages in there. She opened one and put him in.

I had not figured on cages — or on his being all alone. Dr. Thompson sensed what I was thinking. "Don't worry," she said. "Blacky will hang out in the room with him."

But what about food and water? I wanted to know. I told her he'd had nothing since the day before, and who would be there to give him Vittles at 3 A.M.? He'd want them, I knew, and Blacky was hardly up to that. Wouldn't she be there?

Dr. Thompson smiled once more. "No, I won't," she said, "but neither will he want them because he'll be sound asleep too." She opened the cage again. "Now give him an upbeat pat," she said, "and tell him you'll pick him up in the morning — first thing."

I did as I was told. I only hoped he'd believe me. But, before I left, I also patted Blacky. I was so glad he was there.

V ∘ *His Roots*

Dr. Thompson had called me and told me that my cat had come through his operation fine, but, just the same, that night, when he was away, my apartment seemed the loneliest place in the world. It was hard to believe that a small creature whom I had not even known a few days before could, by just not being there, have made it so. But he had — and did.

I resolved to use the time that evening reading everything in my library about cats. I started with famous quotations about them. And, early on, I found one which has since become my all-time favorite. It is by none other than Leonardo da Vinci. "Nature's Masterpiece," he called the cat.

It hardly seemed necessary to go further. Surely that description, by arguably the greatest artistic talent that ever lived — as well as one whose drawings of the cat have never been surpassed — comes at least close to saying it all. But the fact was I soon found others which would become favorites too. One was from, curiously, our own country's preeminent humorist. "If," Mark Twain said, "man could be crossed with a cat, it would improve man, but it would deteriorate the cat."

The English humorist Jerome K. Jerome had roughly the same point of view as Mr. Twain, but he gave his from the animal's angle. "A cat's got her own opinion of human beings," he said. "She don't say much, but you can tell enough to make you anxious not to hear the whole of it."

Here I could not help admiring not only the thought but also the use of the "she" instead of the invariable "he." If Mr. Jerome, 1859–1927, was not talking about a specific female cat, I decided, he was certainly a man in advance of his time.

In any case, to an English art critic, Philip Gilbert Hamerton, I accorded first honors for making what to me seemed the most memorable comparison between those age-old adversaries, the cat and the dog.

"If animals could speak," Hamerton wrote, "the dog would be a blundering, outspoken, honest fellow — but the cat would have the rare grace of never saying a word too much."

When it came to countries, it was not easy to choose which was foremost in praise for the cat. Eventually I decided that France deserved the prize, if for no other reason because it was a Frenchman, Théophile Gautier, poet and novelist, who, albeit immodestly, reduced the contest to totally nationalistic dimensions.

"Only a Frenchman," he wrote, "could understand the fine and subtle qualities of the cat."

A small host of French philosophers were not far behind Monsier Gautier. "Gentlest of sceptics," Jules Lemaitre described his cat, while the oft-quoted Montaigne made the lasting assessment of the cat at play. "When my cat and I," he wrote, "entertain each other with mutual antics, as playing with a garter, who knows that I make more sport for her than she makes for me?"

Still another French philosopher, Alain, was more difficult to understand. "Two things," he wrote, "are aesthetically perfect in the world — the clock and the cat."

I was willing to go along with the cat. But the clock stopped me.

One of the most interesting things I learned that night was the two most common expressions we associate with the cat — that he has nine lives and that he can look at a king — go far back in history. The nine lives, indeed, is one of the oldest of proverbs and has been repeated for centuries. It crops up, for example, in Shakespeare, in no less a work than *Romeo and Juliet*. There Tybalt asks Mercutio, "What wouldst thou have of me?" only to have Mercutio reply, "Good king of Cats, nothing but one of your lives."

A half century ago, a Scottish professor, Sir J. Arthur Thompson, professor of natural history at the University of Aberdeen, wrote a book entitled *Riddles of Science*. In it he devoted an entire chapter to the cat's nine lives. Sir Arthur's thesis was that each of the lives stemmed from one of the cat's lifesaving abilities. The first, for example, Sir Arthur believed came from the fact that the cat always fell on his feet, and that this was the result of his ancestral ability to climb. The second life came from his whiskers, which were a vital part of his ability to operate in the dark and were, indeed, so important to him that to cut them close was, at least temporarily, to incapacitate him.

The third of the lives, Sir Arthur went on, came from the cat's extraordinary ability to smell at great distances, the fourth from the animal's equally remarkable hearing. Despite his small ears, a cat, the professor noted, had proven to be able to turn in the direction of any sound at least twice as fast as the best watchdog.

Sir Arthur declared that the cat's fifth life derived from the animal's amazing visual powers — these eyes having both the legendary ability to see in the dark and also being, in relation to the size of his body, the largest of all animal eyes. On the other hand, Sir Arthur credited the cat's sixth life not to any astounding physical attribute but to the animal's homing instinct — his apparently infallible ability to find his way home, often from long distances and even after a purposeful dislocation. This instinct, the professor felt, was, when the cat lived in the wild, obviously all-important to survival — both from the point of view of the cat's own safety and also that of any newborn kittens which might have been left unattended in the den.

By the time Sir Arthur had reached the cat's seventh life, he, not the cat, was clearly laboring. In any case, he ascribed that seventh life to the cat's ability to make his fur stand on end — more hairs in proportion to body size than can, for example, the gorilla — and thus appear much larger, as well as more frightening, to a larger adversary.

If Sir Arthur was having hard going with his seventh

cat life, he had nothing left at all for the eighth and ninth lives or, for that matter, even what these last two lives were. Having said at the beginning of his treatise that the cat had more than nine lives, he nonetheless leaves us with only seven. Some veteran cat scholars have conjectured that this might have been purposeful — pointing out that while the oriental mystic number is nine, the occidental is only seven. This cat scholar, however, who is no mystic, felt shortchanged.

The saying that "even a cat can look at a king" has, I found, never had the exhaustive treatment accorded to the legendary nine lives, but it too can be traced to an ancient proverb. It has, however, at least one basis in more modern historic fact. In the fifteenth century, the story goes, Maximilian I, of the House of Hapsburg, King of the Romans and soon to be Holy Roman Emperor, was deep in conversation with a friend of his named Hieronymus Resch, a maker of woodcuts. During this conversation, the king looked over and saw that Resch's cat, stretched out on a table, was staring not at Resch but at him. From this rather less than earth-shaking occurrence came, apparently, not only the actual proof of the proverb but also its rather less than happy future connotation — at least as far as kings are concerned. For Maximilian, who spent a good deal of his reign embroiled in turmoil, intrigue, and warfare, always declared that the cat had looked at him with, as he put it, "deep suspicion" — a comment which, once again, will come as small surprise to all the cat-owned, before Maximilian's time, and since.

And, years later the cat and the king confrontation became the basis for one of the famous "Fantastic Fables" of none other than the late Ambrose Bierce:

A Cat was looking at a King as permitted by the proverb.

"Well," said the monarch, observing her inspection of the royal person, "how do you like me?"

"I can imagine a King," said the Cat, "whom I should like better."

"For example?"

"The King of Mice."

Actually, through the centuries, cats have, I discovered, not only looked at kings, they have also lived with them. And, although among kings and emperors as well as among common folk, there has apparently always been both the ailurophile and the ailurophobe, the balance, fortunately for the cat, has been highly in favor of the phile over the phobe. In our own country, while comparatively few of our Presidents have had cats, those who have — notably Abraham Lincoln — were extremely fond of them. Lincoln indeed, on a trip to Grant's headquarters in the dead of winter, and finding there three half-frozen kittens, adopted them on the spot and took them back to the White House.

The other best-known presidential ailurophiles were also, curiously, all Republican — Theodore Roosevelt, Calvin Coolidge, and Herbert Hoover — and, if the latter two at least were perhaps our most conservative Presidents, it should be borne in mind that this trend was not broken by Ronald Reagan. Although it is his dogs which have received most of his animal publicity, the fact remains that he has three cats at his ranch and all three, he maintains, get along not only with each other but also with his dogs.

In other countries, I learned, heads of state have come in both the pro and the anti cat camp. Neither the Kaiser nor Hitler liked cats, but Mussolini, the Tsar, and, curiously, Lenin, were all extremely fond of them. Farther back, Julius Caesar and Napoleon both detested cats, while both Louis XIV and Louis XV loved them. The latter, indeed, having been won over by his queen, Marie Leszczynska, was persuaded to give them the run of Paris.

On the other hand, Henri II, Henri III, and Charles IX were strictly in the phobe camp — indeed, when Charles came to the throne, he is reputed to have several times lost consciousness just at the sight of a cat. Moreover, one of Charles' ministers, Ronsard, went so far as to record his revulsion. "I hate," he wrote, "their eyes, their forehead and their gaze." As for George Louis Leclerc, Comte de Buffon, the famous French botanist who is generally credited with having been the first modern to attempt to embrace all knowledge, one thing he refused to embrace was the cat. "The cat is a faithless domestic animal," he wrote, "that we only keep from necessity in order to use it against another even more inconvenient enemy that we do not wish to keep at all."

But, harsh as these opinions were, I noted that they were strictly minority ones. Popes such as Gregory the Great and Gregory III, Leo XII, and Leo XIII, not to mention Pius VII and the late John Paul, were all pro-cat, and there are many stories of their affection for the animal. When Gregory the Great and Gregory III, for example, renounced all their worldly possessions, each refused to renounce one thing — his cat. And Leo XIII not only befriended a stray kitten born in the Vatican, but made it his companion for life — much of which the cat spent literally curled up in the folds of the papal robes.

In England the cat has long fared very well among the high and mighty. Napoleon might have hated cats, but his conqueror, the Duke of Wellington, was extremely partial to them, as were both Queen Victoria and Winston Churchill. Indeed, under Victoria, England was considered so ailurophilic that, when the Italian ambassador was once asked what he would like to be if he had his life to live over again, he quickly replied, "A cat in London, or a Cardinal in my country."

In point of fact, three of the most famous cardinals in history were also three of the most famous ailurophiles. Cardinal Wolsey, for example, carried a cat in his arms wherever he went and had one eat with him whether he ate alone or sat at a state function. In more modern times Cardinal Newman was, if more restrained, almost as similarly smitten. As for France's Cardinal Richelieu, he was undoubtedly the greatest friend of the cat in history. He had from childhood loved cats and, when he became virtually head of state, he not only made the cat an accepted part of the court but also kept two servants who served no other function but to take care of all his cats. And, on his death, the cardinal provided in his will for the future care of no less than fourteen of them.

Over and over in cat histories I read that, in comparison to other animals, the cat was a very late arrival on the animal scene. Over and over in cat histories, too, I read such a sentence as "The early history of the cat is shrouded . . ." and then, not, as usually ends such sentences, "in antiquity" but rather, of all phrases, "in mystery."

As one now owned by a cat, I hardly found this surprising. So, I irreverently wanted to ask, what else is new? One does not have to be cat-owned for long to know that, if there is one thing a cat loves better than anything else — save, possibly, making a large mess out of something which

had been carefully arranged before he got the.
is a mystery. And if he can, as he so often does, m.
large mystery out of where he has been when you g. .o
look for him, even though he was right there a moment
ago, surely it must have been mother's milk for his ancestors to make a mystery out of where they originally came
from.

In any case, I discovered, late he was. The dog, the
horse, the bear, and the reindeer had, the authorities told
me, been on the scene not just for a short time before the
cat but for a very long time — in fact, for millennia. Furthermore, these authorities point out — and they apparently include the trained bear and the harnessed reindeer
in this assessment — that all of these animals had become,
long before the appearance of the cat, not only the companion of man but also his servant.

The authorities profess their inability to find a satisfactory answer to account for this. Once more, however, even
I, a relative newcomer to the cat-owned ranks, could see
clearly that the answer was staring them right in the face —
the dead giveaway being that word "servant." Indeed, no
self-respecting member of the cat-owned fraternity would
wonder for a moment why the cat's appearance was so
dilatory. Their only wonder would be why, in view of the
situation, he ever showed up at all.

Archaeological authorities point out that, in paleolithic
times, in caves, rock carvings, bas-reliefs, etc., there are
relics and representations of all kinds of animals — from
deer to boar to birds — but not so much as a tooth, a
vertebra, or indeed a trace of the cat. And if this is not
hard enough news for the archaeologists, consider for a
moment the plight of the anthropologists, who have literally gotten almost nowhere in trying to determine the

ancestry of the cat. For centuries they were certain that his ancestor must have been some kind of wild cat but were never able to come up with exactly which kind. Fairly recently, however, flying in the face of the well-worn line that "God created the cat so that man might caress the tiger," they have decided that the First Cat was not any sort of wild cat at all, but might have been some other kind of animal. Indeed, the most recent anthropological evidence to be assembled points to the conclusion that the cat's ancestor was, of all animals, the fox.

One certainly means no disrespect to the wily fox — and it would seem that there are indeed physical as well as behavioral similarities between cat and fox. Just the same, the line "God created the cat so that man might caress the fox" doesn't seem to get the job done.

When and where, then, did the cat first appear? The when was, I learned, no earlier than 3000 B.C. — which is not yesterday as you and I may think of it, but was indeed yesterday when measured by the appearance of a wide variety of other animals. The where was, of all places, Nubia — a word which, ironically, is derived in the Nubian language from *nob*, or slave. Nonetheless, it was in neighboring Egypt, conqueror of Nubia, about five hundred years later, or 2500 B.C., that the cat first came into his own. His first name, in Egypt, was, curiously, "Myeo" — a fact from which, once more, the cat-owned would surely deduce that he named himself. In any case, his rise was rapid. He went from hunter — then, as now, at the low end of the social scale — to guardian of the temple, and, finally, to deity. It was, even by cat standards, remarkable.

The Cat-Goddess was known by a wide variety of names — Bast, Bastet, Ubastot, Bubastis, and Pasht — but whatever she was called, there was no question but that she was very high up in the Egyptian pantheon. She was not only the daughter of Isis, great and good friend of the great God Ra, the principal God of Creation; she was also, in her own right, Goddess of the Sun and Moon. And, although she had to share the sun part of her job with Ra, she was still vital to it — if for no other reason than that the Egyptians believed that, when they looked into a cat's eyes, the fact that those eyes glowed meant that they held the life-giving light of the sun, and this in turn meant that the sun would return the next day. To the Egyptians, who were by no means big on the dark, this made Bast, if not superior to Ra, at least very close to being his equal.

But Bast, aka Bastet, etc., was something else, too. Besides being the Goddess of the Sun and Moon, she was also Goddess of Love. Furthermore, she served in this capacity for both maternity and virginity. And if, in those pre-pill days, this must have taken some doing, she was in any case well rewarded for her trouble. She had her own temple in which she was surrounded by other cats, all of whom were not only also considered to be sacred but who were, in turn, surrounded by priests. These priests both watched over the cats and made predictions and prognostications from them — from, as one historian puts it, "the slightest purr, the faintest meowing, the most discreet stretch or the least alteration of posture."

All in all, it must have been one of the best jobs any animal lover could ask for, but at the time one of the most difficult — particularly since the priests had to give their forecasts to government officials as well as to any and all passersby who merely wanted their fortunes told. One can assume that, good at their jobs as these priests may have been, at least some of the time they must have had to go pretty much on a hit-or-miss basis, just as we do when, for example, our cat disappears and we cannot be sure exactly what is the reason. We do not know, for instance, whether the doorbell is about to ring, or a thunderstorm is coming, or we have just thought of doing something that the cat does not want done — such as giving him a pill or cutting his toenails. And if these speculations are what we have to go on from our cat's complete disappearance, imagine what it must have been like for those priests. Their cats apparently never disappeared — they just occasionally changed positions.

Such a distinguished historian as Herodotus tells us that not only was there a statue of the Cat-Goddess in the various temples, but that there was also a small statue of her in virtually every Egyptian home. "The Goddess," says another historian, "was a disturbing creature whom every Egyptian woman wished to resemble — in the strangeness of her gaze, her slanting eyes, her supple loins, her noble posture and her animal abandon." "Women," says still a third historian, "would rather go out of their way to move slinkily . . . rather like our present-day 'vamp.' And," adds this historian, "Cleopatra herself indulged in this fad."

All of which was to entice, in turn, both Caesar and Antony and which, judged by the success of the musical *Cats*, is still not without its charm today. In any case, Herodotus also tells us that when a cat died in a public place, bystanders would get down on their knees protesting that they were not responsible. Whether this was an act of love or expedience, however, is not clear — the killing of a cat was a crime punishable by death. Cats, like people, were embalmed and mummified and placed in sarcophagi.

It is not surprising, in view of ancient Egypt's attitude toward the cat, that the country's enemies could take advantage of it. When, in 500 B.C., for example, Cambyses, King of the Persians, laid siege to the Egyptian city of Pelusium, his initial attacks were foiled by the ferocity of the Egyptian resistance. Whereupon Cambyses called a halt to these tactics and ordered his men to comb the area outside Pelusium for eight days and pick up, but not harm, every cat they could find. For the next attack, Cambyses had each of his men, as he approached the Egyptian lines, hold up in front of him a live cat. One look at this new development was enough for the Egyptians. Rather than harm the cats, and without any further fighting at all, the Egyptians simply surrendered the city.

It was indeed, I discovered, a cat who was responsible for the ultimate subjugation of Egypt by Rome. A Roman soldier in Caesar's army killed a cat — albeit accidentally. However, an Egyptian mob immediately fell on the man, lynched him, and then dragged his body through the streets. Caesar himself warned the Egyptians of severe reprisals for this action — but the warning only served to further enflame the situation. Virtually all of Egypt rose against Rome in a resistance which continued, off and on, until the deaths of Antony and Cleopatra and until Egypt became a Roman province.

Rome itself was ambivalent about the cat. On the one hand, in the ruins of Pompeii not so much as a single bone of a cat was ever found, and in upper-class Roman homes, although there were all kinds of animals as pets, there were few if any cats.

On the other hand, cats were allowed in the inner sanctum of the temple of Hercules and in performance of the ritual dances to the Goddess Diana. The Daughters of Diana, as they were called, were masked and robed as cats. The Romans did, in fact, recognize the cat's aristocratic aloofness, independence, and freedom from authority. The cat was emblazoned on the standards of many of the Roman legions, and in the Temple to Liberty, dedicated by Tiberius Gracchus, the Roman Goddess of Liberty is represented, somewhat like our own Statue of Liberty, holding a cup in one hand and a scepter, if a broken one, in the other. At the Goddess' feet, however, in contrast to our statue, lies, carefully and gracefully rendered, the sculpture of a cat.

The cat's early history in other countries was also curiously interwoven with legends surrounding the country's religion. In Arab countries, for example, the cat was far better off than most other animals because of a cat named Muezza. The latter, it seems, was the favorite cat of Mohammed, and one day, when he was sleeping on Mohammed's sleeve and the prophet had to leave for a meeting, rather than disturb Muezza, he cut off that part of his sleeve on which the cat was resting. Later, when Mohammed returned, Muezza thanked him and bowed, whereupon Mohammed was so touched that he stroked Muezza's back three times — something which, according to legend, not only gave the cat its eternal ability to land on its feet after a fall, but gave it its three times three or nine lives.

In India, in contrast, all animals were protected by Buddha except the cat — the reason for this being, according to legend, that, when Buddha was dying, all animals were ordered to be present. And all obeyed, except for one — Buddha's own cat.

Here, there are two versions of the story. One has it

that Buddha's cat simply overslept and was late. The other version holds that Buddha's cat was among those present, all right, but that, at just the crucial moment when Buddha was ascending to Nirvana, a rat ran across the temple grounds and the cat, his attention diverted to more earthly matters, pounced on the rat and killed it. This was, of course, an unforgiveable social solecism at an extremely inopportune time. Nonetheless, the cat was eventually forgiven, and today in India the orthodox Hindu religion not only prescribes that each of the faithful "feed at least one cat under his roof," but also rules that, for anyone who kills a cat, "he withdraw to the middle of a forest and there dedicate himself to the life of the animals around him until he is purified" — surely an excellent piece of advice for all "sportsmen."

In Burma and Siam — two areas from which come two of our most famous cat breeds — there were, as in Egypt, cats who had to do with guarding temples and, more importantly, with the transmigration of souls. The soul, it was believed, relived, for a time at least, its existence in the body of a sacred cat before going on to total perfection in the next life. In Japan this belief went farther. The cat had religious significance even after death, and the geisha girls of Tokyo went so far as to raise a fund for a ceremonial service for the souls of the cats which had been killed to provide the catgut for samisens — the banjo-like instruments which they used to entertain their customers. Remarkably enough, before 1602 Japan kept its cats on leashes. In that year the Kyoto government passed a law ordering them released, the idea being that city cats needed their freedom in order to take care of the rats which were destroying the silkworm industry, and that the temple cats needed theirs to keep mice away from the papyrus rolls. Presumably, like all cats before them, and since, they had had, in between mice, a high old time with those rolls.

Ancient China did not actually worship the cat, but cats were strictly bringers of good fortune, because they were living assistants to the Hearth God, the household protector whose image was in every home. One cat was collared and tied in the home, but kittens and other cats were free to go in and out as they wished. Even the collared cat fared well, however, because, true to Chinese tradition for people, the older he or she was, the more he or she was venerated. The Chinese peasant, like the Egyptian, believed in the glow of the cat's eyes at night to ward off evil spirits, but the Chinese carried the Egyptian's fascination with the eyes a step farther. They believed it was possible to tell time this way — that from dawn the pupil in the cat's eye gradually contracted until it became, at noon, a perpendicular hairline. And then, during the afternoon, the hairline's dilation gradually increased until it was bedtime for people and guard time for cats.

Generally speaking, the cat came through ancient history with flying colors — and even through what, to two-legged creatures, were the Dark Ages. The cat's Dark Ages, however, were Europe's Middle Ages. All of a sudden, it seems, all the Eastern superstitions and the legends, even the religious veneration accorded him in the East, were, in the West, turned against him. He became, literally, the creature of the Devil. The Bible, for example, which refers to almost every other animal, has practically no reference to cats, either in the Old Testament or the New. The theory, in regard to the Old Testament at least, is that the Hebrews, having suffered the terrible bondage and persecution which they did under the Egyptians, had no appetite for even the mention of an animal their persecutor had so liked, let alone one which had been so venerated.

When it comes to the New Testament, its ailurophobia is part and parcel of the worst of medieval Christianity. In any case, this kind of Christianity not only removed the cat from its ancestral pedestal but condemned him as the embodiment of the Foul Fiend Incarnate, the intimate source of all manner of witchcraft and sorcery, of voodoo and vampirism, of black magic and even the Black Mass. Along with the Inquisition went just about every cat phobia in the old wives' handbook. Indeed, the Devil's Bible, published in, of all places, France, contained the statement "Only imbeciles do not know that all have a pact with the Devil."

Even the popes were part of the horror, and, all over the Roman Catholic world, as well as through a large part of the Protestant, men and women were tortured and even hanged just for helping or giving shelter to a sick or wounded cat. The superstitions themselves seem to have had to be cruel to be believed. One had it that only the burial of a live cat in a field would insure a good crop, another that only the walling-up of a live cat in a new building would insure the stability of its foundations. Nor was all this stupidity confined to Europe. In the American colonies, no fewer than two thousand accusations of witchcraft involving cats were legally upheld in court.

The black cat, of course, fared worst of all. As the personification of Satan, he suffered the tortures of the damned — literally. An incredible number of black cats were massacred in various ways — not excluding being killed at Mass itself. Cat-burning, indeed, became such an accepted rite that, long after it was a thing of the past, it was defended by Jacques Bossuet, one of the seventeenth century's most famous theologians. Furthermore, his defense was by reasoning which was, unfortunately, typical. Since the practice of torturing cats would have existed in any case, Bossuet maintained, it was better to have it happen during a Christian rite than during a pagan one.

Fernand Méry, French veterinarian and cat historian, managed to find in Brittany one lovely piece of good news for the black cat — a legend which dates from those terrible times but which still exists to the present day. The legend holds that on every black cat there is one hair, and only one, which is perfectly white. If you can find this hair and remove it without being scratched by your cat, you will have a unique good luck charm — one which can render you, whichever you choose — either rich or lucky in love.

But not, apparently, both. In any case, Dr. Méry, in his fine book *The Cat*, concludes his story with a touching comment:

> I particularly like this last legend. It implies that you have sufficiently gained the sympathy of your cat for it to allow you patiently to search through the whole of its coat for this one famous hair. The happiness that can come from this unique white hair is symbolic. It is recognition and reward for whoever can prove so much understanding and goodwill towards an animal that has been for so long despised and ill-treated.

The all-white hair in the black cat legend also sent me scurrying for stories about all-white cats, such as mine.

Once especially venerated, as in ancient times he had been, how had he come through, well, the Dark Ages? I presumed not well because while, in those terrible times, all cats suffered, the all white was so different that, like the all black, there surely must have been ridiculous superstitions associated with him. I did not, however, find any, and in any case, coming out of the Middle Ages, the white cat was soon again, if not a God or Goddess, at least by the time of Louis XV, a court pet. Later Queen Victoria would have her white cat and, in China and Japan, where medieval Christian cruelty had not penetrated, both the Chinese and Japanese emperors had white cats at the same time. Indeed, as recently as 1926, when a new king was crowned in Siam — the grandson of the king of *Anna and the King of Siam* fame — a white cat was carried in the procession. The soul of the king's predecessor was, the belief ran, at least temporarily embodied in him.

For my favorite story of the white cat I am again indebted to Dr. Méry. It happened during World War II in Burma at a time when the fortunes of the Allies in general and the British Army in particular were at a low ebb. The chief British problem was that, to build the strategic roads which they required, they were in dire need of Burmese labor and were willing to pay high wages to get it. But the Japanese, with their superior knowledge of Burmese beliefs and customs, were able to convince these laborers that, in the end, the British would lose anyway. And, the Japanese emphasized, in the meantime, the uncouth British would be making a mockery out of everything the Burmese held sacred — in particular the white, or, as the Burmese called it, the "immaculate" cat. So the road-builders began quitting their jobs in droves:

This went on until an English colonel with considerable knowledge of local beliefs had an original idea. First of all the order went out to all ranks to collect the greatest possible number of white cats. In the meantime, the silhouettes of white cats were stencilled on all the army vehicles, jeeps, trucks, tanks, etc. as if this were the emblem of the British Army. It certainly proved a lucky one. The rumour swiftly spread that the English aerodromes were unassailable, for they were the refuge of the immaculate cat. The same applied to the rolling stock. No more was needed. The native population ignored the Japanese propaganda and gave the full weight of their support to the Allies.

The next morning I was at Dr. Thompson's before any other client. Blacky, I noticed, was not "on the desk."

"No," Dr. Thompson once more anticipated me as I appeared. "Blacky is still with your cat."

As we walked down the hall, she said, "He's fine, but you're going to find he's a little unsteady."

I went in and marched right to the cage. Dr. Thompson was correct. My cat was indeed unsteady — in fact, I would have called him groggy. But, just the same, he had clearly recognized me and was staggering to his feet just as I opened his cage. "Aeiou, *aeiou*," he said.

"Aeiou, aeiou, *aeiou*," I replied, taking him in my arms. "We're going home now."

On the way out, I stopped, either to thank Blacky and hug Dr. Thompson or the other way around — I was too excited to know which. All I did know was that I had my cat again.

VI ∘ *A Difficult Matter*

A few days after the trip to the vet, the
cat and I had our first real disagreement. Or at least it was
the first since our Mexican standoff over the question of
whether or not he would, on occasion and without the
introduction of such an impossible variable to the experiment as food, come when called.

It came over something which, to those of the non-cat-
owned persuasion, would seem ridiculous. It would not,
however, so seem either to any of the veteran cat-owned
or, for that matter, to any veteran cat.

What it was, in a word, was what — entirely irrespective of the question of whether or not he would come to
it — to call him.

Frankly, I was growing heartily sick and tired of telling
people about him and having to do so without the at-
tachment of a name; of having people see him and ask

what his name was and having to tell them, as I had that woman at Dr. Thompson's, that what with Christmas and all, and one thing and another, I had just not gotten around to it; and, finally, of not myself having anything by which to address him properly. I had been using that awful "you" — which is bad enough for a person whose name you have forgotten but is even worse for an animal and is, for a cat, totally impossible.

I was under no illusion that the job would be easy — which, curiously, was something I learned primarily in reverse. In other words, I learned it from the only people who had not bothered me about why I had not yet named my cat or who, when they asked about it, did not ask me its name. They were, of course, the veteran cat-owned and they were far too polite and much too wise to ask such a fruitless question. From them, indeed, I picked up valuable lessons as, little by little, I met more and more of these people and saw firsthand some who had returned, bloody but unbowed, either from the battlefield of an unsuccessful naming war, or from the neutral zone of one in progress. The naming of a cat, like marriage to a person, was obviously not to be undertaken or entered into lightly. On the contrary, it was, as T. S. Eliot, who wrote a whole poem about it, noted, "a difficult matter."

The late Mr. Eliot, I was soon to learn, understated. Indeed, in short order I would also learn that, compared to the naming of a cat, the naming of a baby, a dog, or a book, a battleship, a ball team, or, for that matter, a king, a pope, or a hurricane, is child's play.

Start with a child. You may, for a child, it is true, run into a few minor difficulties. You and your spouse might, for example, be in disagreement, in the case of a boy's name, about the use of Junior and Junior's possible future offspring, of III's, V's, etc., if direct or, if collateral, via an uncle, II's, IV's, etc. You may decide, in other words, that you either don't want to number him or you do. Or you and your spouse may disagree about the use of family names or even about naming your child after a family member — which will depend, of course, upon your liking or dislike of the party in question, or perhaps even upon such an ignoble consideration as that of a potential will. You may also have a second thought about some name you at first liked because of the possibility of a highly unsuitable nickname which might later be bestowed upon the child because of it by some unfeeling schoolmate.

But, as I say, these are basically small problems, and you and your spouse have, after all, nine months in which to talk them out, discuss them with wiser heads and, ultimately, solve them. And, best of all, after you have made your choice, you will not face even the most remote possibility of a squawk from your namee — at least not until long after it is far too late.

So much for the child.

Next take a dog. Even to consider comparing the difficulty of naming a dog with that of the naming of a cat is a waste of my valuable time, and yours too. Your dog will accept any name. Furthermore, he will recognize it almost at once and on the second or at most the third call will not only come to it but actually run to it. Above all, your dog will never, either by look, sniff, sneer, or innuendo, criticize your choice. You, as his master or mistress, as the case may be, have made your decision and he will abide by it. If that is what you want, then it is what he wants, too, and that is all there is to it.

The naming of a book can be a bit trickier. But, once again, to think of it in the same breath with naming a cat is — well, you can simply take my word for it that I have done both and there is no comparison. Many years ago, I was fortunate in having as my literary agent Miss Bernice Baumgarten, one of the most distinguished in the book field. One day I addressed to her the question of how important she thought a book's title was. She answered peremptorily that it was of virtually no importance. I next addressed to her the question of what she thought was a good title. "Any title," she replied, equally peremptorily, "of a good book." After that, I decided not to bother her any more about the matter.

The other examples I cited also fail to measure up in difficulty to the naming of a cat. Battleships and ball teams are, after all, named, if the former, for individuals or states; if the latter, the first part of the name reflects location, while the second part is usually concerned either with such mundane matters as a local occupation (cowboys, oilers, brewers), or evoking the image of something fierce (giants, bears, raiders), or even something as simple as the color of their sox. As for kings and popes, they are not really named at all — rather, like the juniors previously considered, they are numbered. Finally, although hurricanes used to present a reasonable challenge when female names only were employed and when there was the danger, in years in which there were a lot of hurricanes and the difficult letters toward the end of the alphabet were approaching, of running out of names not previously used, nowadays, with the addition of male names in deference to male liberation, anyone could do the job — even that awful new weather man on your local TV.

The naming of a cat, on the other hand, is something entirely else again. A cat who dislikes his name can, and

I am reliably informed, often does, go through his entire lifetime without ever, even by a careless mistake, acknowledging that he has ever heard it before, let alone recognizing, in any perceptible manner known to humankind, that it could in any way have any possible connection with him.

Early on in my name quest, a friend of mine who, with her husband, lived with a dozen or more cats, told me that, when all her cats were together and she or her husband called one of them, the others would often turn and look at the cat called — but, at the same time, while that cat would occasionally return the stare of the other cats, he or she would never look at or respond to her husband or her. The story was proof positive, she maintained, that cats have no real objection to other cats' names, they just object to their own. Another friend of mine, the copyeditor, as a matter of fact, of this book, well recalls two Siamese cats she once had, each of whose sole acknowledgment of their own names was to register extreme jealousy when the other was even discussed, let alone called.

All the cat-owned will agree that cats can be finicky about a great many things — about their food, for example, about certain people they either like or dislike, about noise or weather or almost anything else you or, more importantly, your cat can think of. But all of these are basically finickinesses which develop over a period of time and which therefore at least allow you the opportunity to develop your defenses against them. Your cat's persnicketiness over his name, however, begins with the very first time you are rash enough to try it on him.

An extraordinary number of cats indeed seem to harbor the firm belief that they should be able to exercise strict editorial control over their names and to employ, if need be, wartime censorship. Nor is this belief confined to the question of whether or not they like or dislike certain names. Rather it is based on a far more fundamental matter — and that is, in sum, that they are by no means sold on the idea that they should have a name to begin with.

Actually, I learned there was only one rule of thumb you could really count on about a cat's attitude toward your choice of name. And this was that, whatever you expected its attitude to be, it would be precisely the opposite. Some years ago a friend of mine, Jane Volk, rescued, in Palm Beach of all places, where her husband was a distinguished architect, one of the toughest tomcats I ever saw in my life — a fighting tom who had one eye, one and a half ears, half a tail, and a battle-scarred face. Of all her cats, her friends were sure, this would be the most difficult to name. Mrs. Volk, however, elegant and serene, promptly dubbed the cat "Mother's Precious Treasure." Not only did the cat not object, he took to the name immediately. It was always my belief that he knew it was funny too.

Some years ago, Eleanora Walker, a distinguished cat rescuer, wrote a whole book about the subject, entitled *Cat Names*. Mrs. Walker asks in one chapter, "Do our cats name us?" She answers this in the affirmative, and then states that these names probably have to do with humans as providers. "My former husband," she writes, "swore that Humphrey and Dolly and Bean Blossom called me The Big Hamburger."

In another chapter, however, Mrs. Walker goes a good deal farther. In this, entitled "The Tibetan Way," she tells us that she asked a friend of hers who was, as she puts it, "more spiritually advanced" than she, to work out a "method of meditation" which would "help someone bring forth the cat's name."

The friend dutifully did so:

> Relax yourself by lying on your back on the floor with your knees raised and your feet firmly on the ground. Breathe gently and regularly, concentrating on the exhale, and try to clear your mind of clutter. . . . If you are new to meditation and distractions continue to bother you, repeat the following mantra silently to the rhythm of your breathing. *Ham/Sah. Ham* on the inhale and *Sah* on the exhale.

This was apparently the method by which Tibetan mystics who "want to attain the qualities of a particular deity" got themselves in shape for the task ahead — in other words, for trying "to reproduce the image of the god in all its complexity inside themselves." And Mrs. Walker tells us encouragingly, "If you've ever seen a Tibetan deity, you'll realize that this is no mean feat. A cat is easy by comparison."

I was willing to take her word for it. The second and final step was just around the corner:

> My friend recommends that you look closely, intently and lovingly at your cat, observing every little whisker and eyelash and the details of his markings. Then, having relaxed yourself and cleared your mind as much as possible, close your eyes and try to visualize your cat in perfect detail. Sooner or later the essence of your cat's personality will reveal itself to you, and a name will rise from the depths of your subconscious to fit it, and that will be the best possible name you could have chosen for your cat.

Mrs. Walker's book was published some time after I had to name my cat. And so, unfortunately or perhaps fortunately — as a Bostonian, my long suit has never been Tibetan mysticism — I did not have the advantage of it. Nor, for that matter, did I have her list of possible names for white cats. These were, in two columns, as follows:

Whitey	Vanilla
Snowy	Whitewash
Snowhite	White Cloud
Snowflake	Blanche
Snowball	Bianca
Snowdrop	Daisy
Snowflower	Ivory
Snowfire	Rinso
Snowman	Soapsuds
Ermine	Marble
Eggshell	Crystal
Eggwhite	Jack Frost
Eggcream	Oyster

I have no wish to offend anyone who owns a white cat with one of those names, but frankly I didn't see the slightest chance of my cat sitting still for a single one of them.

What I did carefully consider, on the other hand, was an historical name. After all, I was primed with research on the subject, and I saw no reason why my cat should not be the proud bearer of the name of one of his ancestors.

I started with Bast the Egyptian. The trouble was that Bast was not a God but a Goddess. I didn't want to be sexist about the matter of naming, and Bast sounded as if it could be male, all right, but still, there was something a little unnerving about unsexing a Goddess. Leo XIII's cat curled up in the papal robes also appealed at the outset. The pope had named that cat Micetto — a name I liked. But here I was stymied by the fact that it was not only a long story to tell anytime anyone asked me why I had picked that name for my cat, it was also an odd one for a Boston Episcopalian. My Episcopalianism is High Church, all right, but it is hardly in Micetto's class.

The third name I considered was Mohammed's Muezza. Once again, however, the story I would be forced to tell over and over was a long one. And, more important, although I was partial to the Prophet himself, I was considerably less so to many of his present-day followers who, among other failings, have failed utterly to follow his teachings on the matter of kindness to animals.

The names of two of Cardinal Richelieu's cats briefly appealed — Perruque and Racan. They had been named by the cardinal by virtue of the fact of having been born in a wig — i.e., perruque — one commandeered for the occasion by His Eminence from the head of the Marquis de Racan. But the marquis, I learned, was, besides being a friend of the cardinal, not only a minor poet but a bad one at that. If my cat was to be named for a poet, it would only be, I decided, either for a major one or at least a good minor one.

Two other famous cats in history were intriguing. One was the cat owned by Shakespeare's patron, the Earl of Southampton, who was imprisoned in 1602 by Elizabeth I in solitary confinement in the Tower of London. The cat, a large black and white fellow, had been the earl's constant companion and somehow made his way to the Tower and, by climbing down the chimney, to the earl's cell. From here he refused to move and, when the earl was finally released, one of his first acts was to commission a window in Welbeck Abbey. The window is still viewable today, and it shows the earl, alone in his cell, with, beside him, his faithful cat.

The other cat was perhaps Italy's most famous feline — one who had lived in the late 1880s and the early 1890s in a café in Venice in the square facing the church of Santa Maria Gloriosa dei Frari. Not only was this cat an all-white cat, but he was also so well known that a book of his friends was kept in the café, and in it were such signatures as Pope Leo XIII, the king and the queen of Italy, Prince Metternich, and Tsar Alexander III. Furthermore, after the cat died he was immortalized by a sculpture which, like the Earl of Southampton's window, still exists.

There were just two troubles with these cats as possible purveyors of a name for my cat. They were, in order, first, that there was no known name for the Earl of Southampton's cat, it having been lost in history, and second, although the name of the cat in the Venetian café had not been lost, this name turned out to be Nini. And this was one I could see my cat rejecting out of hand.

Two more recent English cats also seemed worthy of consideration. One was Queen Victoria's best-known cat, which, once more, had the additional appeal of being white. The good queen had even found a name which was, apparently, to both her and the cat's liking — White Heather. I could not, however, see it for mine. The other possibility was Winston Churchill's well-known wartime companion Nelson. Much to his owner's chagrin, however, during the London blitzes, Nelson was invariably to be found, if at all, ensconced under the farthest corner of the nearest bed. "Despite my most earnest and eloquent entreaties," the prime minister commented, "I failed most utterly in persuading my friend before taking such craven action to give even passing consideration to the name he bore."

There were many interesting stories about the cats of literary giants — but few, alas, had apparently taken enough time in their naming to suit my purposes. Samuel Johnson, for example, was so fond of one of his cats that, according to Boswell, he invariably left the house to get the cat oysters each afternoon, rather than order one of the servants to do so. Johnson was apparently convinced that, had he so ordered the servants, one of them might well have exacted some sort of vengeance on the animal for having to perform such a menial task. Evidently, despite what you read about servants in those good old days, all was not always beer and skittles between upstairs and downstairs. In any case, the cat's name turned out to be Hodge — one fine, perhaps, for an English butler, but not, in my judgment, for an American cat.

The name of the cat of Alexandre Dumas the Younger came closer to my ideal. This cat, whose name was Mysouff, would every day walk with M. Dumas to a point halfway between his home and his office and then return home. And always he would come back to that place to meet his master and walk home with him. More extraordinary, on days when his master had another engagement and was not going to be there, Mysouff somehow knew and, according to Dumas himself, would never leave the house for the rendezvous.

Mysouff was, I decided, a name I would try on my cat — long story or no long story. Another possibility was one of Charles Dickens' cats, or rather kittens. When Dickens was working late in his study, this kitten would climb up on his desk and, with her paw, snuff out the candle. Dickens would usually relight it, whereupon the kitten would immediately snuff it again — after which Dickens would cease work for the night and devote his attention to her. The trouble was that, once more, I could not find out the name of the kitten. Along with two others, she had been born in Dickens' study to a cat whom, when he first saw her and before he found out she was a female, Dickens had named William. After learning she was about to become a mother, he renamed her Wilhelmina.

Alas, I decided, I could not have a namesake of my favorite author. Dickens would have to go. I did, however, find another possibility. It was a cat owned by H. G. Wells, and its name was Mr. Peter Wells — one which Mr. Wells, the author, not the cat, always insisted be used with the "Mr." included. In any case, Mr. Peter Wells was assuredly one of the most remarkable of cats. When a guest talked either too loudly or too long, it was his, Mr. Peter Wells', custom to jump down from his favorite chair, and then, making as much noise and getting as much attention as possible, proceed to leave the room. This surely must have added a dimension of suspense that has rarely been equalled in any salon, and I would, I decided, at least try on my cat the name Mr. Peter Amory.

Of all authors and cat-lovers I found, Mark Twain certainly has the distinction of having given his cats the oddest names. Among these were Apollinaris, Zoroaster, Blatherskite, and Sour Mash. The idea was, Twain maintained, not to be mean to the cats but, since they were so difficult about names anyway, to go all out and give them names which would be good practice for children learning the pronunciation of long and difficult words. Twain also had a cat named Tammany, one of whose kittens provided in Twain's poolroom the same appraisal service offered by Mr. Peter Wells in H. G. Wells' drawing room. It was the habit of the kitten to hole up in a corner pocket, thus adding, by her blockade, a new dimension to any game. To this tactic she added a second with her habit of not always, but occasionally, when the mood struck, swiping out with her paw and redirecting a ball headed toward the other corner pocket. In these cases, Twain recalled, house rules called not for any condemnation of the kitten but merely for putting the ball back as closely as possible to the original position and reshooting the shot.

Last but not least I uncovered the startling fact that undoubtedly the greatest cat-lover of all authors — the French writer Colette — was also one who failed so miserably at the naming of her cat that she ended up calling her *La Chatte*. It was, of course, merely the feminine of the French word for cat. While Colette always frankly admitted to having tried and failed to find any other name satisfactory to La Chatte, she was nonetheless highly pleased and always stoutly defended her cat's eventual choice. "I believe," she said, "that all cats like to think they are the only cats in the world. If this is true, then La Chatte at least has the firmest nominal claim on the honor."

Colette's name for her cat made another point. Our word *cat* is actually closer to other languages — and in those languages closer to ours — than perhaps any other common noun. He is *chat* in French, *Katz* in German, *ga'ta* in modern Greek, *cattus* in Latin, *gato* in Spanish and Portuguese, *gatto* in Italian, *kat* in Dutch and Danish, *katt* in Swedish and Norwegian, *kot* in Polish, *kut* in Egyptian, *kat* in parts of Africa and *katsi* in others, and *kott* in Russian. Even in languages in which he is a little different, he is still close — as in *kedi* in Turkish and *gatz* in Armenian — and elsewhere where he is different, the word for him comes from the sound he makes — as in *mao* or *mio* in Chinese, *neko* in Japanese, *biss* in Arabic, and, perhaps simplest of all, in Indonesian, *puss*.

There were at least possibilities here — of giving him the name for himself in another language — and, after some consideration, I placed on my list both Chairman Miow and King Kut. I also made a last run at literary catdom, all the way back to the first known reference to a domesticated cat in literature. He belonged to an Irish scholar in the ninth century, and his name was Pangur Bán. I liked the P and B — good easily recognizable consonants — and I put Pangur Bán on my list too. Elsewhere, however, the pickings were slim. There were, among non-fiction cats, Poe's Caterina, Thoreau's Min, Hemingway's Puss, and D. H. Lawrence's Puss Puss, and there were also, in fiction, Saki's talking Tobermory, Don Marquis' alley cat friend of Archie, Mehitabel, Gallico's resurrected goddess Thomasina, and even H. Allen Smith's Rhubarb, the cat who inherited a ball team. But none, unfortunately, filled the bill.

I also gave due consideration to the names of the great cartoon cats of history — among them Felix, Tom (of Tom and Jerry fame), and Garfield. If Garfield was my favorite name, however, the story of Felix interested me the most. Drawn by Pat Sullivan, an Australian cartoonist who came to this country in 1914, Felix' name, which derived from "felicity," was specifically chosen to counteract cruel superstitions about cats. Also, Sullivan admitted, he had based Felix in no small measure on the movements and humor of Charlie Chaplin. In any case, Felix became so famous that when Walt Disney created his Mickey, whom he had at first wanted to be a cat also, he soon decided that rather than compete with Felix, he would make Mickey a mouse.

Alas, Felix was black. But in the course of my search I did discover a truly remarkable white cat, who also had an equally remarkable name. He was Don Pierrot de Navarre, and he was owned by the French author Théophile Gautier, the same man whom we have previously met as the author of the statement that only a Frenchman could appreciate a cat. Gautier wrote movingly about this animal, who must surely rank at the top of all the literary cats in history:

> Sitting close to the fire, he seemed always interested in the conversation, and now and then, as he looked from one speaker to another, he would give a little protesting mew, as though in remonstrance to some opinion which he could not bring himself to share. He adored books and whenever he found one open on the table, he would sit down by it, look attentively at the printed page, turn over a leaf or two and finally fall asleep, for all the world as if he had been trying to read a modern novel. As soon as he saw me sit down to write, he would jump on my desk and watch the crooked and fantastic figures which my pen scattered over the paper, turning his head every time I began a fresh line. Sometimes it occurred to him to take a part in my work, and then he would make little clutches at my pen, with the evident design of writing a page or so. . . .

Now there was a cat I could identify with — and so, I hoped, could my cat. Or that at least he would do me the courtesy of giving to the name of Don Pierrot de Navarre the consideration it so richly deserved.

The cat was lying in my lap with his head on my knees sound asleep. But since it was getting late and I had no idea how long our naming session would take, I decided to wake him up and get on with the job.

Gently I turned him around with his head facing me. Then, after giving him a moment or two to pull himself together, I began, slowly but firmly, our discussion.

All animals, I explained, when they are domesticated and live with people, have names. Even birds who have lived with people, I continued, have names. I wanted to get his full attention as quickly as possible, and he is very interested in ornithology.

Just the way, I went on, people have names. The way, I proceeded a step further, I had a name. My name, for example, I told him, is Cleveland.

He gave me a long look which seemed at first to be full of concern, but, I soon realized, also contained advice. It was clear he felt I should, and as quickly as possible, seek professional help.

I ignored this. Instead I told him, just as firmly as I had started, that if he would keep an open mind about the whole thing, having a name would not only make him feel more comfortable around people, it would also make him feel so around other animals.

Even animals who were not domesticated, I pointed out, who just lived near people, such as animals in zoos, had names. Very large animals like elephants and lions and tigers and leopards. In fact, all large cats had names. And so, I said, did — well, smaller cats.

I paused meaningfully and then proceeded. All cats who lived with people, I pointed out to him, had names. Not just some cats, not just most cats, but *all* cats. Indeed, I concluded fearlessly, if he could name one single solitary cat who had ever lived with any person anywhere and who did not have a name, I would agree not to name him. Furthermore, I would even give him a reasonable time to think of such a cat.

And I did, too. I played it absolutely straight. But when he did not come up with a solitary example, as I knew he would not, I moved ahead to my peroration. In most cases, I told him, people just decided on a name they wanted to give a cat, and the cat itself had nothing whatever to say about the matter. I told him that I was not one of those people, and I would certainly never do a thing like that — I had much too much respect for him. Instead, what I was going to do — in fact what I had already done — was not to name him anything until I found a name that I — and here I almost slipped but managed to catch myself — that *he* and I, I quickly amended, *both* liked.

His tail began thumping on my knee. He wanted me to get to the point. The point was, I said, that I was going to give him fair say in the matter. In other words, I was going to try various names on him and get his reaction to them. And here I gave him fair warning. If he was willing to cooperate, well and good. But if he wasn't, so be it. In that unhappy event, I would just have to take the one which he appeared to dislike the least.

With that I put him down. All right, I told him, I am now going to turn my back on you and walk a few steps away. And when I turn around, I want to see what your reaction is.

I did so. "Here, Don Pierrot de Navarre," I said. "Here, Don Pierrot de Navarre." I then turned around to see the reaction.

I couldn't believe my eyes. If it is possible for a cat to

look daggers, then my cat looked daggers as perhaps none of his brethren had ever looked daggers before. I could not imagine what could be the matter. Certainly Don Pierrot de Navarre was a beautiful name, stately and imposing, fully worthy of any cat's dignity, almost royal . . . and then I stopped. It was, of course, nothing to do with Don Pierrot de Navarre. What had happened was that, in my enthusiasm to try and sell him the name, I had used the forbidden word "here." I had indeed marched straight into the anti-come danger zone and thus I had broken our previous compromise agreement.

I apologized profusely. I told him that I fully understood it would be impossible for him even to consider the merits of any name which had been prefaced by such an offensive and obnoxious word as *here*. But would he listen to it again? Without, of course, that word?

He would — and did. This time I just said, "Don Pierrot de Navarre" as persuasively as I could, and then once again repeated it.

And this time his look was just plain blank. And a blank look on a white cat is, I assure you, a very blank look indeed.

I decided to abandon Don Pierrot, at least for the moment, and move on to the works of Alexandre Dumas. Once more I turned my back. "Mysouff," I said, "Mysouff." I liked the *f* sound and was sure that he would, too. "Mysouff," I announced a third time, and emphasized the *f*.

I got a reaction, all right, but not the one I had been hoping for. Instead, the cat made a beeline for the kitchen. Obviously to him I was discussing dinner. When I had persuaded him to return I abandoned literary pretensions and chose, for my third try, the first of recorded domestic cats. "Pangur Bán," I informed him. "Pangur Bán."

For the first time I got a reaction. Not a large reaction, mind you, but a small one. I made a mental note of it, but forged ahead anyway. "Mr. Peter Amory," I intoned as if I were a butler announcing a guest; "Mr. Peter Amory."

What I received this time was a very slow, very large, and, I thought, very deliberate yawn. Alas, I regretfully concluded, I was not destined to have a cat named for such a stern editor of guest conversation. But the attempt to get Mr. Peter at least partway by him had given me the idea for another possibility. For some time I had been known as a curmudgeon. And the more my cat and I had been together, the more I detected unmistakable signs of curmudgeonly behavior in him. Whether he was modelling himself on me I couldn't yet be sure. But I flattered myself that he was, and anyway I thought Curmudgeon deserved at least a try as a name.

There were, however, a couple of difficulties here. For one thing, I had learned at first hand that *curmudgeon* is a word the meaning of which is a mystery to a large number of young people nowadays — who are, of course, the very people most in need of such a man. And I say "man" advisedly — a curmudgeon is one of the last things in this world a man can be that a woman cannot be. I had one aunt who tried all her life to be a curmudgeon and who never succeeded. All she did succeed in doing was making my uncle a curmudgeon. In any case, when I once asked the studio audience during a television appearance what a curmudgeon was, the first definition I received was "a medieval weapon," and second was "a kind of fish."

There was also that matter of the prefix "cur" — which was bad enough from a dog's point of view but from a cat's obviously totally unsuitable. And then it came to me. Why not change the "cur" to "purr." Purrmudgeon — surely an excellent name for a cat of mine and never mind if some young people thought it was a weapon or a fish.

Eagerly, I tried it on him. "Purrmudgeon," I said, pronouncing both *r*'s, and then, lest he think I was gilding the lily, I tried it again without any emphasis on the second *r*. "Purmudgeon."

He rejected it, of course. And the most maddening thing was that he had never seemed to me more curmudgeonly than when he did so. Discouraged, I returned to the drawing board. Perhaps, I mused, I was too abstruse in my choices, and the whole process should be simpler. It was a long way from the kind of thing I had been throwing at him, but I decided to have a go anyway. What about the name of Christmas for him? The night I had found him had, after all, been if not actually a white Christmas, at least a white Christmas Eve.

I tried it, as usual, twice, "Christmas. Christmas." Again, nothing. I had the uncomfortable feeling that he was now too bored even to yawn. And I was beginning to get very cross. What on earth could he have against Christmas as a name? Furthermore, Christmas was a terrific name because it was full of easily understood consonants and *s*'s — which any cat worthy of the name would understand by, if nothing else, the hissing sound.

"Christmas," I hissed. "Christmas."

He understood, all right. His ears went straight back and he hissed right back at me. I decided to concede.

I had, however, one more suggestion to make. Would

he consider the name Santa Claus? That was a name, I told him frankly, that even someone as persnickety as he was could not possibly have anything against. Santa Claus was, I explained, not only a jolly fellow, full of good cheer who brought joy and gifts, but he was also someone — something which I knew would appeal to him — about whom everybody made a great mystery. Older children, for example, were not allowed to tell younger children there wasn't any such person. And, as a final inducement, I assured him, if it would make him more comfortable with the name, we could spell it Santa Claws.

It was no use. He didn't want to be Santa Claus no matter how it was spelled. With some deliberation he rose to his feet, stretched himself paw by paw, and then, with a look which said more clearly than words that he had taken as much of this nonsense as he could reasonably be expected to absorb at one sitting, he marched sedately from the room.

I stayed where I was. I had been determined to have a new name for him by nightfall or know the reason why. Now I knew the reason why.

I plunged into thought. History had failed, humor had failed, the holiday season had failed. What was left? For some reason I started to think what some of my very favorite animals were — perhaps I could get a name from among them. I was in no mood to include the cat, but I did include the dog, the horse, the donkey, the tiger, the dolphin, the otter, the beaver, and the bear. There were many others but, suddenly, with the bear I stopped. Bear would be a good name for him, I thought — he looked like a little bear. And, since he was white, what about Polar Bear? As I thought of it, I remembered that he had at least reacted slightly to the name of Pangur Bán. It was an omen. They were both P. B.'s.

I tracked him into the bedroom, where he had curled up comfortably on the counterpane. I did not come right out with the name. I had learned a good deal from my previous earnest attempts. This time there would be no big deal. "Oh, Polar Bear," I remarked, "there you are." I said it so casually that he could not possibly have had a clue as to what I was up to. I sat down on the bed and began to scratch him. "Well," I said with the same casualness, "how's Polar Bear?" I went on from scratching to scrubbling and scrumping.

What I was doing, of course, was making it a fait accompli. And although I would like to tell you that he looked directly at me and solemnly nodded at me, he of course did nothing of the kind.

I would also like to be able to tell you that from that moment on he knew his name and that, if he doesn't always come to it, he does at least some of the time. As I say, I would like to be able to tell you that, but it would not be the truth.

Finally, I would say that, whether he knows it or not, Polar Bear has turned out to be the perfect name for him. But that too would not be the truth. There is only one perfect name for a cat. And, as T. S. Eliot has told us, it is one we will never know:

The Naming of Cats is a difficult matter,
 It isn't just one of your holiday games;
You may think at first I'm as mad as a hatter
When I tell you, a cat must have THREE DIFFERENT NAMES.
First of all, there's the name that the family use daily,
 Such as Peter, Augustus, Alonzo or James,

Such as Victor or Jonathan, George or Bill Bailey —
    All of them sensible everyday names.
There are fancier names if you think they sound sweeter,
    Some for the gentlemen, some for the dames:
Such as Plato, Admetus, Electra, Demeter —
    But all of them sensible everyday names.
But I tell you, a cat needs a name that's particular,
    A name that's peculiar, and more dignified,
Else how can he keep up his tail perpendicular,
    Or spread out his whiskers, or cherish his pride?
Of names of this kind, I can give you a quorum,
    Such as Munkustrap, Quaxo, or Coricopat,
Such as Bombalurina, or else Jellylorum —
    Names that never belong to more than one cat.
But above and beyond there's still one name left over,
    And that is the name that you never will guess;
The name that no human research can discover —
    But THE CAT HIMSELF KNOWS, and will never confess.
When you notice a cat in profound meditation,
    The reason, I tell you, is always the same:
His mind is engaged in a rapt contemplation
    Of the thought, of the thought, of the thought of his name:
        His ineffable effable
        Effanineffable
Deep and inscrutable singular Name.

VII ∘ *His Hollywood*

To this day it is not quite clear to me
why I decided to take Polar Bear with me on that trip to
Hollywood. One reason was that I was going to be gone
at least a couple of weeks — which was actually longer
than the total period I had had him. Although Marian
would, I knew, come in and not only feed him but play
with him as well, still he would be alone a good deal of
the time — and at the very time when he should be for-
tifying his security, not feeling deserted.

The second and more important reason for taking him
was one which I would not admit, even to myself. It was
the simple fact that I had become so fond of him that I
simply could not handle being without him that long.

I was well aware of the difficulties attendant on my
decision — indeed, I had been made so by every cat friend
I had. One and all imparted such dire warnings about

feline foraying that, after listening to them, I became convinced that a cat, unless trained at kittenhood, ranked as a fellow traveller on long trips somewhere above alligators and orangutans, but well below cross servants, quarrelsome children, sick goldfish, and compact automobiles.

There were, these friends were quick to inform me, many reasons for this. In the first place, they pointed out, cats, perhaps more than any other species, were territorial creatures — their home was their castle, their hearth, their heath, and even where their heart was. In the second place, these same friends emphasized, cats were creatures of conservatism and tradition. My friends did not go so far as to claim all cats were Republican, but the fact is that I had for some time suspected it of Polar Bear. For one thing, he didn't like anything happening that had not happened before. And although this had little to do with political party affiliation, it was a prejudice which, of course, flew fairly in the face of trip-taking — particularly on a plane to a place where he had never been before.

I patiently listened while my friends informed me that, in the third place, I would soon find that a cat regarded anywhere he had never been before, even a relatively simple hotel room, as strictly uncharted wilderness, around any corner of which lurked dangers which would put to shame a Chamber of Horrors in a wax museum on Hallowe'en. By no means satisfied with a total tailing, tracking, and sniffing of every nook and cranny of such a place, my cat would, they assured me, remain stiffened with terror until he had been there for a long enough period to have monitored every single sound from outside the room as well as inside, and to have carefully cased all comings and goings, both by day and night. They added, as a kind of minor afterthought, that during such a period my cat would, of course, not eat anything for as long as it took to convince me that he would never eat again — as being his way of administering fit punishment for the worries to which I had subjected him by taking him to such a place to begin with.

In the fourth and final place, my friends firmly abjured me, I would have the problems of the actual trip itself. Cats, I was informed, love scenery and seeing things, but these sights must be contemplated while they themselves are stationery. When they themselves are being fast-forwarded, they do not have the slightest interest in even the most engrossing visual fare — such as birds flying by outside the window of a car, train, or, for that matter, even a plane. If forced to watch same, I would, in fact, find not only disinterest but actual distrust and distaste, both of which would undoubtedly culminate first in severe motion sickness and finally actual vomiting.

As if all this was not enough, manuals on cat travel were presented to me which were crammed from beginning to end with a veritable litany of peregrinational pit-falls. One manual advised that the worst thing possible before taking one's cat on a long trip was to take him on a short or trial one. "This," I read, "will only make you worry more." Another manual declared that no trip with a cat should be undertaken without water, a non-spill water container, a litter pan, litter, air freshener, disinfectant, a whisk broom, and a supply of moist tissues. The latter, this work advised, are "for you, not the cat."

The worst possible thing, I read, was even to consider taking one's cat either to a friend's house or a hotel room. Dazedly I wondered what other alternatives there were. In any case, I was advised, the house of a friend, particularly a friend not sympathetic toward cats in general, let alone the specific problems of a cat on tour, could prove a nightmare. As for a hotel room, I read that literally no hotel room could be secured, that, sooner or later, a maid or a bellboy or an errant room service waiter or engineer would open the door and your cat would fly out, both to escape the new enemy and to find you — and while he would indeed be looking for you, your chance of finding him, when he could literally be anywhere, would be infinitesimal.

To all such reasoning and advice, I turned the deafest of ears. Pish, tush, I thought. Polar Bear was different. To one of my friends, who was most severe on the subject of the perils of the road, I addressed the question as to whether or not he happened to be aware of the fact that a kitten had once climbed the Matterhorn. A kitten, I repeated. He looked at me as if I had two heads, but he did not stop me from telling him the story.

It had happened some years ago. Matt, as he has since been renamed, was at that time a ten-month-old kitten — a black and white one, I was pleased to note — who had been with his owner the night before the climb in a hotel at the bottom of the mountain. The next morning Matt's owner awoke before dawn, and, weighed down with climbing equipment, departed the hotel room, leaving Matt behind to await his master's return. Step by tortuous step, Matt's owner and his party, together with guides, compasses, and a full complement of mountaineering tackle, including ropes, pickaxes, food, water, and emergency medical kit, made their long trek toward the summit. Finally they reached it and, as they were basking in their achievement and congratulating one another on their collective hardiness, the celebration was suddenly interrupted by a loud and querulous meow. Up the 14,780 feet behind them, also every step of the way, including up sheer rock, but with of course no equipment, food, or water, had come Matt — who, they soon learned, was very hungry and very thirsty but otherwise not the slightest the worse for wear.

I pointed out to still another skeptic some other extraordinary travelling which cats had accomplished. The best-known story, perhaps, was that of the "incredible journey" described in the great book of that name by Sheila Burnford. Miss Burnford, it should be remembered, not only wrote movingly of the trip across three hundred miles of Canadian wilderness of two great dogs — the young Labrador and the brave old English bull — but also told the tale of Tao, the Siamese cat who more than once saved all three of them, including both dogs. Indeed, on one occasion he saved them from a large and furious mother bear whose cub they had disturbed.

Finally, I told my skeptic friends of what I believe is still the all-time record for the longest journey ever made by a deserted animal. This was that of a cat owned by a New York veterinarian. The man lived with a friend and, when he had to move to California, he left his cat, believing that the animal would be better off staying with his friend in his old and accustomed quarters. The cat had been to the new house, in California, just once, but, five months later, that vet, like the Matterhorn climbers, heard a familiar meow. He opened the door and although his cat was indeed the worse for wear, he nonetheless dignifiedly entered the house, made his way to the familiar armchair which had been in the previous house, clambered up onto the cushion, and promptly fell asleep.

Surely, I told my friends, if one cat, as a kitten, could climb the Matterhorn, another could help two dogs make it to safety across the Canadian wilderness, and a third, alone, could travel the three thousand miles from New York to California, I could at least take Polar Bear along with me on one measly little trip to Hollywood.

Today, looking back, I would like to say how right I was. And, of course, how all the people who had warned me had been wrong. The only trouble is that it did not turn out that way. They were right and I, hard cheese as it is for a man of my mettle to admit, was wrong.

Actually, the trip started out fine — although I would like to make it clear that I have never understood those ridiculous airline rules which allow for only one animal in the first-class section and one in tourist. Are they afraid of barking, or meowing, or fighting, or people tripping over them, or what? The animals are, after all, in carriers, and provided each is separated by a row, having at least a few more per flight would hardly seem a major menace to air travel — at least not on a par with having the person in front of you putting his seat back in your lap, or having four armrests for each row of three people.

Although I had once done an imagined interview with the designer of airplane tourist sections — a charming fellow, albeit one only three feet nine in height and with only one arm — the fact was that I was hardly in a position to make a fuss about the animals in the passenger section. The Fund for Animals had, not long before my flight, been one of the leaders in the battle to force the airlines to redesign their baggage compartments so that they would be more humane for animal travel — which, up until our fight, they had not been — and for me now to carry the fight immediately to the passenger sections, with my own personal cat, seemed a bit much.

The long and short of it was that I had no alternative but to obey the regulations — and so I had obediently, and well in advance, secured one reservation for Polar Bear and one for me. I also had the proper kind of carrier, which, though a tight fit, could just make it under the seat. And the flight attendant could not have been nicer. Before takeoff, she allowed me to open the carrier enough so that she could have a quick pat, and she generously ooohed and aahhhed over how beautiful he was. She also promised that I could, after takeoff, open the carrier again.

However, not only did Polar Bear not return the young lady's generous advances, he pointedly and unceremoniously turned away from her. This is a peril, I was learning the hard way, of introducing your cat to anyone when you and he are in transit. The fact is that most cats, most of the time, have already met everybody they care to meet. And when they are travelling, make no mistake, all cats have. It thus behooves the cat-owned, on the road, to have at the ready a small arsenal of excuses, not excluding anything from little white lies to large black ones.

I made use of one of the latter. I told the flight attendant that ordinarily Polar Bear was the soul of friendliness, but having had the tranquilizer and all — well, she would understand. She didn't, of course, and he hadn't, but at least I had tried.

I was lucky in one respect. I had secured the window seat and there was no one in the middle seat. There was, however, a large man in the aisle seat and he had watched with interest Polar Bear's meeting with the stewardess. "He isn't much of a traveller, is he?" Once more I lied. I informed the man that Polar Bear was a great little traveller on short flights, but on long flights — which, I explained, he apparently suspected this was going to be —

he was inclined to get sick. This information, I was fairly sure, would minimize the man's interest when I would later be able to get the carrier up on the middle seat between us. And it did.

As we roared down the runway, Polar Bear gave voice to a steady stream of woeful "aeiou"'s — all of which were clearly audible even above the roar of the plane. I reached down and poked a finger through one of the airholes in the carrier to reassure him. But I doubt if it did much good. At that moment, compared to air travel, he would clearly have opted for a Conestoga wagon climbing through the Brenner Pass. To him airplanes put too many people into too small an area, and in the particular area where he was, there were many too many feet, which is his least favorite part of people at any time. Besides, it was all terribly noisy, cramped, and uncomfortable and, in his opinion, dangerous.

When I finally had his carrier up on the seat beside me, with the top partly open and my hand inside and resting on him, I tried to reassure him about the danger. But I wasn't very convincing. As an old pilot, I don't like takeoffs either — and I know they are, with the ghastly exception of running into another plane while airborne, the most hazardous part of flying.

I tried to interest him in the clouds outside the plane window, but he found them poor visual fare. It was obvious that everything my friends had said about cats not liking to be moving while doing their sightseeing was right on target. Even if Polar Bear had seen a bird, I knew it would not have had the slightest appeal. As far as he was concerned, everything out there was for the birds.

The arrival of food, I hoped, might at least distract him from his current dim view of the world in general and me in particular, but once again my friends were right. Though the flight attendant brought him his own little dish of food when the peanuts and drinks came, he wouldn't even get close enough to it to see what it was. As for the rest of the meal, he just wasn't buying. Airplane food was, to him, airplane food — and its appearance served only to reinforce the fact that the fast about which I had been warned, and which I dreaded, had, in fact, begun. I realized that I should have had a can of his own food to tempt him with, and indeed I had several such cans with me. But where were they? Like a selection of his toys, of course, they were in my suitcase — in the bowels of the baggage compartment. I think of everything.

The worst part of it all was that he had clearly not only gone on a hunger strike, he had also gone on a sleep strike. And when a cat does that, you can be sure the news is all bad. That trip lasted five and one half hours, and it seemed, at a minimum, like that many days.

At last, however, it was over, and I was met at the airport by Paula Deats, a screenwriter and former Fund coordinator. Paula is a cat woman from way back and she was over Polar Bear like an enthusiastic tent. Polar Bear, on the other hand, while better than he had been during the flight — anything, after all, was an improvement on that — was reserved. We were not even out of the airport yet, Paula was the first California girl he had met, and frankly, he seemed to feel, it was all, as it so often is in California, a bit too much too soon. Once more, it was time for an excuse. "He hasn't slept much," I told her, "and he's got a little jet lag."

Paula had managed to park close by, itself a feat at the L.A.X. Airport, and we were soon on our way — albeit in an automobile which, I was too polite to mention, could easily have fit inside the ancient Checker which I drive in New York. I have always regarded it as interesting that California girls who apparently feel very deeply about the necessity of having their own "space" somehow have so little regard for it in their vehicles. Nonetheless, crowded as we were, I opened the carrier and let Polar Bear out. I made no effort, however, to lift him onto my lap and show him the sights of L.A. Indeed, I was determined not to do so until we had turned onto Sunset Drive and left the horrors of the Freeway behind us.

"When are you going back?" Paula inquired. "Oh," I replied, "in a couple of months." It was an old routine between us. It had long been my experience that nowhere but in California do people ask you about your return immediately upon your arrival. Californians in general, I have noticed, are at least somewhat prone to this practice, but with California girls it is nothing less than second nature. They have, after all, been trained at birth that if they fail to insert this question into the conversation well before any plans are made, an out-of-towner, ignorant of local customs, might actually be tempted to stay through one of their sacred weekends — and hence interfere with either meditations or hot tubs, est or Rolfing, windsurfing or hang gliding.

Polar Bear, during this exchange, was alternately thrashing around or pretending he was dead. However since Paula, like most animal activists, had been known to house the worst-behaved animals imaginable — particularly her cats — I decided that rather than try to make further excuses for him, I would instead take the offensive. I told her that a fellow author, Richard Smith, had recently written an entire article about the difference between East

Coast cats and West Coast cats — and that, in his opinion, East Coast cats were less concerned about their looks than West Coast cats and preferred to be valued for their minds rather than for their bodies alone.

Paula refused to rise to the bait. I was, however, not finished. I told her that while Smith also stated that having a meaningful, caring, and nurturing relationship might be more important to West Coast cats than meeting a cat with a great body, the fact remained that East Coast cats *always* preferred to select their partners on the basis of personality and shared interests.

Paula said nothing. I only hoped, I further ventured, that Polar Bear's neutering would not interfere with any future inclinations he might have toward nurturing.

But Paula, being, like Marian, used to my bad jokes and worse puns, still refused to rise. I tried to get her to hold hands with me with her free hand, but she made a fist. I repeat — California girls are very strange.

As for Polar Bear, getting him, on this drive, to rise to anything was no easy task either. Finally, once we had swung onto Sunset, I was reduced to picking him up, planting his bottom on my lap, and putting his paws on the closed window. "Look, Polar Bear," I exhorted. "California! Beverly Hills! Movie stars!"

To Polar Bear this was once more evidence that I had gone around the bend — in this case some three thousand miles around. In any case, he did not see any movie stars, but he did see many people selling maps to movie stars' homes, as well as a steady stream of well-manicured lawns and an occasional well-manicured native either getting in or out of a well-manicured foreign automobile. He also saw a number of joggers and runners and was, like all sightseers in that area, interested in the fact that it is all right to run or jog in Beverly Hills, but you can be arrested for walking.

The Beverly Hills Hotel, toward which Polar Bear and I were headed, was a hostelry to which I had regularly repaired since the days of *High Society*, the first movie script I had ever worked on. Originally, the area where such late notables as Will Rogers, Spencer Tracy, Douglas Fairbanks, Sr., and Darryl Zanuck had played polo — from which derives the title of its famous lounge — both the hotel and the town around it were named after, of all places, the obscure Boston resort of Beverly Farms. Why it should have been so named — as well as why the "Farms" part became lost — is not clear. Nor, to an old Bostonian — one born, in fact, at the equally obscure Boston resort of Nahant — has it ever been quite clear why Californians, no matter how strange, chose to name their most select location, as well as their most renowned hostelry, for a Bostonian resort whose chief claim to fame is the fact that President William Howard Taft once stayed there. Certainly Beverly Farms was not even as famous as the Boston resort of Lenox — one forever memorialized by its headline of January 6, 1933 — "PRESIDENT COOLIDGE DEAD — MAY HAVE FISHED HERE."

But Beverly Hills is far from California's only example of curious naming. Indeed, I learned on the impeccable authority of my friend Maria Cooper, daughter of the late Gary, that the most famous of all California towns was named by a man who, visiting in London, was so taken with his host's name for his house that, upon his return to California, decided similarly to favor the area in which he owned land. The name was Hollywood.

Beverly Hills never became as famous as Hollywood,

but one of its hotels did indeed become better known than any of Hollywood's. And it did so despite the fact that it was, and still is, one of the strangest-shaped edifices this side of Xanadu — and was, and still is, painted pink.

The reason for its fame was simple. Early on, the hotel was not just a place to see, but, far more important by Hollywood standards, a place in which to be seen. All of this, too, started modestly. Indeed, there are still old-timers who recall the first of its mandatory sights — an elegant stallion being ridden down "The Bridle Path," as it was then known, by an equally elegant white-haired character actor named Hobart Bosworth.

Mr. Bosworth was not to remain for long in solitary splendor among the scenic sights. To the hotel repaired not only the Garbos and the Valentinos, the Barrymores and the Charlie Chaplins, the Barbara Huttons and the Howard Hugheses, but also royalty and Presidents, moguls and magnates. And while this parade of notables would, because of the worldwide penetration of the silver screen, have made any hotel famous, the Beverly Hills Hotel was made particularly so because of the penchant, on the part of a goodly percentage of its patronage, to choose the place not only for their regular visits but also for their irregular trysts. Following the footsteps of such as Clark Gable and Carole Lombard came, without benefit of clergy, either to the hotel proper or to its even more secluded bungalows, literally dozens of other celebrated couples. And yet, conversely, when other illustrious couples came unexpectedly with benefit of clergy, these often proved to the average sightseer, perhaps by sheer contrast, to be even more exciting — as, for example, when Mr. Howard Hughes suddenly appeared with an apparently bona fide Mrs. Hughes. And when Mr. Hughes and the former Miss Peters not only took separate bungalows but also ate all their meals apart, this only added to the thrill — particularly when it became known that the Hugheses, after ordering by room service, spent their entire mealtime talking to each other on the telephone.

What had always attracted me to the Beverly Hills Hotel was less the high jinks of the Hollywood hierarchy there than a far simpler and far more practical matter — the hotel had always, from its very opening, been known for hospitality toward animals. Indeed, in many cases its animal guests were almost as famous as were their human owners. Elizabeth Taylor holds, I believe, the record for having, through the years, brought the most animals to the hotel — she also holds the record for bringing the most husbands — but the one-visit record is held by Robert De Niro. Arriving for the filming of *The Last Tycoon*, Mr. De Niro brought with him seven cats.

In those days, animals had their own registration card at the desk and were accorded service on a par with all guests. The only time indeed when service faltered was when a maid refused to clean the bathroom of the fourteen-year-old son of the Ali Ipar of Turkey. In the bathtub, according to the maid, was a bear cub which was not only larger than she was but also had never been properly registered.

Today the policy of the hotel toward animals has, along with its changing ownership, altered. And it has done so not just with such animals as bear cubs but with dogs and cats. It no longer admits, let alone welcomes, them. I have never understood this — or indeed understand why any hotel refuses its guests the right to bring pets. If, for example, one has a dog which barks at night or menaces people in the elevators, it is reasonable to be asked to leave. But if, on the other hand, you have a well-trained dog, he should — perhaps for an extra fee and even the signing of an agreement to pay for any damage the pet might cause — be welcome. By the same token, if you have a cat which claws the furniture, you should, upon your departure, be charged for same. But if you have an animal which is not destructive, he or she should be welcome. All first-rate European hotels take pets, with this policy, as a matter of course. In this country, however, the current trend, with a few notable exceptions, such as the Holiday Inns, which take pets unless it is against a state law, is unfortunately in the opposite direction. One can only hope that in time and with the increasing respect being accorded pet ownership, this trend will be reversed. A possible sign is the success of the Anderson House, a hotel in Washaba, near Minneapolis, where not only are cats welcome but, if you have not brought yours and are homesick for him, the hotel maintains fifteen of them in a barracks dormitory with their names over their rooms, from which you can select a companion to share your room for the night. "It all started," Jeanne Hall, granddaughter of the hotel's founder, told me, "when a man from Pennsylvania, recuperating from a severe operation at the nearby Mayo Clinic, missed his cat so much I lent him one of mine. Now we have so much demand for them we need more. We even have honeymooners who ask for them."

Fortunately, when I arrived with Polar Bear at the hotel, it was still a pro-animal era. Actually, I was engaged in stuffing him into his carrier when Smitty, the doorman who has been there since before anyone (and sometimes even he) can remember, opened the car door. "Hello, Mr.

Amory," he said. "What have you got for us this time?" He peered into the carrier. "Oh," he said, "just a cat." I forgave Smitty. The last time I had arrived at the hotel for a Fund benefit, I had had with me a cheetah — one owned by the actor/writer Gardner McKay and one which, up on the dais, when suddenly flashbulbed from behind by an aggressive photographer, had whirled about so rapidly that, although my arm had been hit by just the very end of his tail, so quick was his motion that at first I had thought my arm was broken.

After the desk amenities were concluded, Wayne, my Bostonian bellman friend, came forward to take the luggage and, on the way to the room, to discuss with me the future fortunes, or lack of same, of the Boston Red Sox and the New England Patriots. Wayne, like me, is a lifetime sufferer.

Once in the room, after Wayne had gone and I had checked all screens, I opened the windows and let Polar Bear out of his carrier. I expected at least a bound around and "At last we are here!" sort of thing. Instead I got exactly what my friends had said I would get — total suspicion. His most motion was, in fact, owl-like — a swivel turn of his head toward the dark closet and under the bed. In vain I explained to him that no enemies could possibly lurk herein — they could not afford the prices. By then, however, he had lost all confidence in not only my judgment but also my credibility.

For some time he did nothing. And when, after what I regarded as a reasonable period, I could stand this no longer, I leaned down, picked him up, carried him to the windowsill, and plumped him down on it. Following this, I moved his head in the direction of the lush California greenery, the handsome pink bungalows across the way, the fascinating sprinklers, and even the interesting tennis game in progress on the courts below. He would have none of any of it. Indeed, except for one short nose wrinkle — which I took to mean he had at least deigned to notice that there was a different smell to California — I could not even get him to continue looking out. And the moment I released him he flew off the windowsill. Then, slowly and warily, he began his policing of the area. The telltale sign of this whole procedure was not only his tail itself — which wasn't up or even reasonably level but was, on the contrary, so far down it was close to dragging — as was indeed the rest of him. Indeed, he conducted the entire search as if he was crawling.

I pretended to scold him. There was absolutely no reason, I informed him, for his slithering around like a wounded bug. Of course he ignored me. When he had finally satisfied himself that there were no immediate enemies inside the room, however, he next did exactly what my friends had warned he would do. He went rigid — this of course to monitor every passing sound in the corridor outside the room, of which, unfortunately, there were many. From time to time, when there were definite evidences of such outside movement, as for example a hall carpet sweeper, he would turn and look at me. Was I just going to sit there, or would I do something about it? Was I an ally or was I at best a defector and at worst a mole? Why had I brought him to this den of iniquity anyway?

To distract him, I unpacked his food, prepared some for him, and put it down with a bowl of water. When I had done so, he again just looked — first at the food and then at the water and finally at me. Obviously he had not the slightest intention of eating or drinking anything. Was this then, I thought darkly, the continuation of the fast of which I had been warned and which he had begun on the airplane? I refused to believe he would do such a thing to me. I did not, however, refuse to believe it so surely that I did not resort to something of which I totally disapprove. I took him over to the water and literally slurped some into him. His look told what he felt. So now, he was saying, reeling back from the shock, you intend to drown me? I told him I had no such intention — he could go without eating for as long as he pleased — but he would jolly well not go without drinking and that was that. Even Gandhi, I reminded him, took liquids during his fasts. And with that I pointed to the water and gave him to understand that if he would not take a drink, I was fully capable of slurping him again.

Amazingly, he did take a drink — albeit a very small one. Actually, I thought, as I savored this small victory, I could use a drink myself. And so, without further ado, I moved his food and water to the bathroom, made a makeshift litter box, and then picked him up and put him in there. I was about to leave when he gave me one more of his looks.

This one was a truly remarkable one. It was the look that a boss gives a worker who is leaving at four-thirty. It was a look which also asked whether or not I, in all seriousness, thought that I was now going to put him in prison — to put him in a place from which he could not possibly even guard the door? Surely I must have taken leave of the last few senses I had left.

I refused to argue. His position, I told him, simply did not merit debate. I also informed him that where I had placed him was hardly a prison. After all, it had an open window from which, even with the screen, he could see all the sights outside and furthermore, there was even a telephone by the commode. He looked once more at me and then at the floor. Where was he expected to lie down? Surely not on that cold, bare floor? I decided to give in on this minor point, and reached for the bath mat. There, I said. And then, trying to make a big thing of it one way or the other, I closed the door.

"AEIOU," he said, and said it with fervor. Indeed, it was such a piercing remark that I was sure it could be heard on the tennis courts below. But I refused to be swayed by it. Instead, I took a sheet of paper from the desk. I was determined, as all the cat travel books had suggested, that there be not just one but two safeguards — both the "Do Not Disturb" sign, which I would place on the outside of the room door, and, on the bathroom door itself, a second and perhaps more potent sign. "PLEASE DO NOT OPEN THIS DOOR UNDER ANY CIRCUMSTANCES," I wrote. "DANGEROUS DOG INSIDE."

As I proudly propped the sign against the door, I could not help thinking that if the son of the Ali Ipar had come up with such a masterpiece, his bear cub might never have been evicted. I tried not, however, to think what Polar Bear would have thought about it.

Actually, with the exception of Polar Bear's attitude toward the entire experience, my trip could not have been more successful. The trip had two purposes, and both were connected with one of the Fund's major wars — against the clubbing of the baby seals. The event occurred each March in Canada off the ice floes of the Magdalene Islands in the Gulf of St. Lawrence and on the so-called Newfoundland Front. I had been on the ice many times and seen the clubbing firsthand. It took place only a few days after the birth of the snow-white infant seals and happened right beside their mothers, who, in a seal's natural environment, the water, would have been strong adversaries, but who, on land, where they had to remain until the seal pups were old enough to swim, were powerless to defend them.

It had become obvious that, in this battle, not only were we not getting anywhere in Canada, we were now actually losing ground because Canada was carrying the fight to us. The same government officials and Fisheries officers who either kept us off the ice entirely or who arrested us when we did manage to get there were now trooping to the United States in a public relations blitz which included radio and television appearances and meetings with the editorial staffs of influential newspapers. Over and over, these Canadian emissaries repeated the same message — that the poor people of the Magdalenes and Newfoundland were utterly dependent on the funds obtained from selling seal pelts, and, as for the clubbing itself, it was not only not cruel, it was actually much less cruel than the killing of animals in an American slaughterhouse. The facts of the matter, which these emissaries ignored, were, of course, much different. The poor people of the Magdalenes and Newfoundland got no meaningful money at all — indeed a mere pittance — from the clubbing compared to the profits reaped by foreign commercial sealers. As for the comparison with American slaughterhouses, this conveniently ignored the fact that non-kosher slaughter in this country, regulated by the Humane Slaughter Act, employs not clubs or hac-a-pics but stunning bolts to render the animals unconscious before death. Nonetheless, the blitz went on and indeed even grew in scope and intensity until it reached the point at which Brian Peckford, then Canadian minister of fisheries and later premier of Newfoundland, told a nationwide U.S. audience that, to Canadians, the clubbing of seals was much the same as was, to Floridians and Californians, the picking of oranges.

One thing was certain — that January we definitely needed some kind of victory in this war. So far the strongest thing we had going for us — and the thing which in the end would win the war — was film. Indeed, one of the Fund for Animals' firsts — and one which I particularly treasured — was that we had managed to get on network television some remarkable footage of the clubbing.

Actually, we had been lucky. The footage was so grim that, try as we might, we could not at that time even get it on a major local station, let alone a network. Finally, however, on the old ABC Dick Cavett morning interview show, I succeeded — primarily because the show was going off the air anyway, and either none of the network brass bothered to look at the film to see if it might be upsetting to the viewing audience, or if they did, didn't care. So air it did, and caused enough stir so that again mostly by luck, that night it was picked up and aired once more, as filler on a slow news night, on the ABC network news.

The effect of this film on millions of American viewers was extraordinary. Mary Tyler Moore, for example, one of the first notables to support us, told me that she remembered exactly where she was and what she was doing when she saw it. "We were at our beach house," she remembered. "I was standing outside the kitchen door and I was holding a pot of soup. I'm not exactly the flamboyant type," she continued, "but I was so horrified, and so angry, that I just threw that soup against the wall.

Then I called our local station and asked them how I could get in touch with you.''

Miss Moore was not the only notable who felt that strongly. Another was her late Serene Highness Princess Grace of Monaco, who soon became the Fund's international chairperson. "I cannot stand the idea," she once told me, "that wild animals are killed to satisfy fashion." The baby-seal clubbing became a cause not only for her but for her whole family — the young Princesses Stephanie and Caroline even going so far as to take petitions out onto the streets of Monaco to try and get passersby to sign in protest against the killing.

Doris Day was, and still is, in many ways the most important supporter of all. The first national chairperson of the Fund, she would meet me at a health-food store in Beverly Hills for what she termed a "healthy breakfast." Doris would arrive by bicycle after her regular early morning round of looking for strays, and I remember, at one of these breakfasts, asking her if she believed that love of animals was inherited. "I know mine was," she told me. "My mother was in on the very first rescue I ever made.

"We were living in Cincinnati," she continued, "and I was very young. The people next door had a big, young dog outside in their yard, and I loved him very much. Then, one weekend, his people went away and left him, in very cold weather, to fend for himself without any food or water. I never forgot it, and I never spoke to them again. The dog cried and cried and the second night we took him in. And then, the next day before they got back, we took him away to my uncle's house and never said a word. They believed he had gotten out of the yard and run away, or maybe been stolen. And," she ended fiercely, "he had the greatest life with my uncle — that dog. He had the greatest."

Doris' first love then, and still now, is stray and unwanted dogs and cats, but she had also made for the Fund for Animals, along with Mary Tyler Moore, Angie Dickinson, Amanda Blake, and Jayne Meadows, our famous "Real People Wear Fake Furs" anti-fur advertisement, and she felt, if anything, even more strongly about the clubbing of the baby seals.

Altogether, we had put together quite a group of anti-clubbers — a group which included Henry Fonda and Jimmy Cagney, Cary Grant, Katharine Hepburn, Dinah Shore, Jimmy and Gloria Stewart, George C. Scott and Trish Van Devere, Jack Lemmon and Felicia Farr, Glenn Ford, Burgess Meredith, Jonathan Winters, Steve Allen, Burl Ives, Art Linkletter, Beatrice Arthur, Jean Stapleton, Yvette Mimieux, and Joan Rivers.

Many of these stellar names turned out for the press conference which was my major reason for being at the hotel and, after it was over, a number of them worked with me to make anti-sealing public service announcements supporting our position. Moreover, those of them who were also painters — and an extraordinary number were — gave us one or more of their works for us to sell and raise funds for our campaign. Henry Fonda, for example, brought me a painting he had done — a beautiful study of a rose in a vase on an autumnal windowsill — wrapped in an overcoat. "It won't sell around here," he told me. " 'Round here they know I'm not that good. You'll get more for it out of town."

Mr. Fonda was far too modest. He was a fine artist, as no less an authority than Andrew Wyeth once told me,

and we later sold his work for a large price. As for Kath-arine Hepburn, she not only gave us a painting to sell —
a wonderful and lacy study of two young actresses in turn-of-the-century costumes — she also allowed us to make prints from it. It was, she told me, a picture she had painted in "a very happy time" — when she and Spencer Tracy, in between film-making, used to paint together.

I thought of Polar Bear often during the press confer-ences and visiting with our notables. Upstairs and alone, imprisoned in the bathroom, he had of course no part in most of the proceedings. But, with two of the notables, he did play a part. One was a remarkable animal activist named Paul Watson.

Paul and I had been corresponding for some time about the kind of activism we needed to let Canada know we still meant business in the war against sealing. What we had decided upon, in a word, was to paint the seals — to paint them with a red organic dye, one which would be harmless to them but would render them useless for furs.

Our meeting was to decide how best to do this. When Paul arrived, Polar Bear took an immediate liking to him — perhaps, I decided, because Paul looks rather like a bear. Large in size as he is, however, Paul is strictly the "Gentle Ben" kind of bear. And as he sat patting Polar Bear at his feet, he told me briefly the story of his life. A Canadian, he had, at the age of eight, written a letter to another Canadian friend of mine in New Brunswick, Aida Flem-ming. Mrs. Flemming had founded, for children, a "Kind-ness Club" and it was to this, for membership, that Paul had written.

He had grown up, it seemed, in an area where some

children regularly shot birds, tied tin cans to the tails of dogs and cats, and put frogs in the street to see how many would be hit by cars. First Paul would protest, then, if his protests were not successful, he would physically intervene. He was often beaten up, but he was never beaten down and, as he grew older, he thought a lot of other things were also worthy of intervention. In sum, not for him were the ways of the hunters who hunted, the trappers who trapped, or, now, the sealers who sealed.

At the outset of our meeting, we both agreed that because of the extraordinary protection the Fisheries officers and even the Royal Canadian Mounted Police gave the sealers — from the air as well as by ship — our options to accomplish our objective were few.

One was to go in by parachute. Both of us agreed, however, that this would be an extremely difficult and dangerous operation. Paul pointed out that it would involve parachute training for all the "painters," and also that they would have to come in at night — which meant not by helicopter but by fixed-wing plane. He felt that this could be done using the most modern "soft" landing chutes, which were capable of being accurately steered and could even hover, but he also pointed out that we would still face the possibility, if not the probability, of some of the painters landing not on the ice but in the ice-cold water, in which case their survival time would be minimal. Finally, it was my turn to note that even if we were successful in getting a team in by parachute, I didn't see any way of getting them out. The ice was too craggy and uneven and far too rapidly changing to count on a rendezvous point, and the seals were spread over far too wide an area.

In the end, we decided to rule out parachute-painting altogether, and went on from there to discuss our second option. This was to try to paint the seals from a plane — by using a crop duster which would be low and slow-flying. I told Paul we had located a pilot who felt, by flying in from Maine at night, that he could do the job, and that we had even gone so far as to have him make some practice runs on some tame sheep outside Denver. But, as with the parachuting, I told him, there were problems. At best, flying in and crossing in the Canadian border at night, with no filed flight plan, would subject the pilot to permanent loss of license — at worst, there was a good chance he would be shot down. I also told Paul that from the practice runs we had had, we had ascertained that both accurate control of the dye as well as its direction had proved next to impossible. We had not hurt any sheep, but there was a very good chance that, considering the winds and weather conditions over the ice at night, we could even blind some seals. And, even if we did not, after it was over the authorities would surely publicly announce that we had done so.

All in all, the plane option too was ruled out. This left us with only one final option — to go in by ship. The major problem here was that it would have to be a ship capable of getting through the ice, which could often quickly freeze, solid as granite, to incredible depths. The commercial sealing ships had their way to the seals literally carved through the ice for them by huge Canadian Coast Guard icebreakers — we would have to do it alone. I knew that the price of buying an icebreaker would be far beyond us, and I asked Paul if it would be possible to charter one. He shook his head. But I refused to give up. I told him, as an old salt from 'way back — one who had spent his boyhood summers in Marblehead, Massachusetts, birthplace of the Revolutionary hero General Glover, the country's first Marine — I simply was not convinced that somehow, somewhere, we could not get hold of some kind of ship which could, by hook or by crook, get through to those seals. I told Paul I wouldn't presume to tell him, a former Merchant Mariner, what kind of a ship it would be, but I did want him to tell me if my idea was at least possible.

Paul said it was, and for the first time I saw light at the end of our tunnel. Paul too became excited. He told me that he felt there was no need for us even to think in terms of an icebreaker. That we should, in his opinion, just buy a regular ship and make it into an icebreaker. How, I wanted to know. "By," he said firmly, "putting concrete into the bow, and a lot of rocks, too."

I like people with answers. What kind of ship was he talking about? Paul suggested a British trawler. The British fishing fleet, he said, was in deep trouble, and he felt we could pick up a trawler relatively cheaply.

I leaned over to pat Polar Bear, who was still at Paul's feet. What kind of money, I asked nervously, were we talking about? It was Paul's turn to pat Polar Bear again. "Maybe a hundred thousand dollars," he said, "maybe two hundred thousand."

Paul's long suit, I would soon learn, was not economics — and particularly not economical economics. The Fund for Animals had, at that time, a grand total of less than half that amount. I would have to raise a lot of money, and quickly, and — because we would have to maintain secrecy about what we intended to do — I would have to do it all without being able to tell people what their money would be going for.

It was not a pleasant prospect. Nonetheless, the success of our press conference had made me optimistic. After a moment's pause, I told Paul to go to England and get us a ship as fast as he could. Then, as we were shaking hands at the door, I added something else. I told him I would like to name the ship *The Polar Bear*.

Paul looked downcast. I asked him if he didn't like the name. He shook his head. Well then, what was it? Paul shuffled his feet. "I already had a name in mind," he said. "I wanted to call her," he went on, "*Sea Shepherd*."

I had to admit that his was the better name. I looked at Polar Bear. "But why," Paul asked, "don't you bring Polar Bear along? Every ship needs a ship's cat — you know, for good luck."

This was no time for travel lies — little white or large black. I told Paul I would talk to Polar Bear about the matter, but for him not to count on it. Polar Bear, as he surely could see, wasn't much of a traveller. If he wasn't any too fond of Hollywood and the Beverly Hills Hotel, he could hardly be expected to be thrilled at the prospect of banging through the Canadian ice, in a ship which wasn't designed for the job, in twenty-degrees-below-zero weather.

While we were still at the Beverly Hills Hotel, however, Polar Bear did at last get to meet a movie star, and it was eminently fitting that, when he did, it turned out to be one of the greatest of them all.

It was Cary Grant, and it happened in a curious way. I had for some years known Cary and occasionally saw him when I was in California. On this occasion I had invited him to have a drink with me in the Polo Lounge. I had assumed that this hallowed Hollywood room would have, through the years, had enough stars as to be in its way a "safe house" in which there would be no such thing as autograph seeking or other untoward events of that nature. But I had reckoned without the truly incredible appeal of Mr. Grant. Hardly had we sat down when at least three people had left their own tables, come over to ours, and were just standing there.

Cary never gave autographs, but his turn-downs of requests for them were such studies in charm that I often thought they served as come-ons even to people who knew they wouldn't actually get one. In any case, this proved itself on this occasion — and, as usual, Cary was up to the challenge. To one woman who gushed, "My friends will never believe I met you unless . . . ," Cary gently interrupted, "You mean you have friends like that? You really shouldn't." To a man who began, "I hate to bother you, but . . . ," Cary's interruption was firmer. "Don't ever," he advised, "do anything you hate." And finally, to a third man, who started, "My wife will kill me . . . ," Cary was also admonitory. "Tsk, tsk," he smiled. "You really shouldn't have that kind of a relationship — it's too dangerous."

Even when the autograph seeking had abated, we were not out of the woods. A woman suddenly appeared, glass in hand. "I just want," she said, on the way past me, "to sit in his lap." While I was sure that Cary would be up to a charming rebuff even to this request, there was, however, something about the woman that so irritated me that I rose, seized her arm, and made an effort to stop her. At this, the man who was with her at the table from which she had come and who was also doing well in the drink department, suddenly rose. "Take your hands," he shouted, "off my wife!"

Cary, who I am sure had been responsible for such scenes for well over half a century, thought the whole thing was funny. I did not. Nor did Nino, the Polo Lounge longtime maître d'. He hustled over and, with stern finesse, soon had the situation well in hand and the act over. Rather than risk a return engagement, however, I suggested to Cary that we adjourn our meeting to my room. And thus it was that Polar Bear got to meet his first movie star.

On the way to the room, Cary told me that he had always been a dog man himself and that frankly he always thought people who loved cats were a little "barmy," as he put it, on the subject. After we had entered the room, however, and Cary had sat down, and I had gone over to the bathroom to give Polar Bear his unconditional release, a remarkable thing happened. Polar Bear made a beeline for Cary and promptly jumped up in his lap. I gave Cary the age-old pet owner's story, which in this case was the truth, that it was the first time I had ever seen Polar Bear do that with a stranger. I also asked him if he wouldn't admit it was at least a better deal than the woman downstairs.

Cary, patting Polar Bear, proceeded to ask me some questions about cats. He wanted to know, for one thing, if I thought it was true that in general women like cats and men like dogs. I replied that it was the generally held theory but there was some evidence, a bit of which he was patting, that this situation might be changing. He also asked me if, again in general, male cats were more friendly than female. I said that I thought this was also true, again on the evidence before him, but I thought it was a theory we had best keep to ourselves. "It's the same thing, really, when you get right down to it," Cary grinned, "with people, isn't it?"

In his last years, Cary did have cats, and although people were inclined to attribute this to the fact that his wife Barbara was a cat person, I always thought Polar Bear deserved at least some of the credit.

VIII ∘ *His Fitness Program*

Polar Bear and I were, from the beginning, two very different individuals when we were sick. When I am sick, I want attention. I want it now, and I want it around the clock. Besides this, I wish everyone within earshot of my moans and groans, of which I have a wide variety, to know that I am not only at death's door, but also that I have the very worst case of whatever it is I think I have which has ever been visited upon man, woman, child, or beast since the world began.

If, for example, I have a slight cold and my cold has taken a turn for the worse, I wish people to gather around my bedside in respectful silence. For those with poor hearing, I wish them to gather especially close, and for those with poor memories, I wish them to bring pad and pencil — so that, of course, they can take down and transmit to posterity, exactly as I have uttered them, hoarsely and with extreme difficulty, my last words. In much the same manner I visualize my loved ones gathering, after I have gone to my final reward, to hear my Last Will and Testament. In this I intend to give them further instruction, after I have gone and they no longer have the benefit of my counsel, on how they are to conduct themselves.

If, on the other hand, my cold is a little better and there is now a fighting chance that I may, entirely due to my heroism in the crises, eventually get well, then I also wish them to gather around in the same manner and tell me how wonderful I have been through it all and how desolate they have been at the thought of coming so close to losing me. At such times I like to warn them that, during my convalescence, on pain of relapse, they must be constantly on call twenty-four hours a day — that they should think of themselves as army orderlies, always at the ready to bring on the double whatever it is of which I most have need — be it food or drink, books or magazines, a chess player or a chess computer, as well as, of course and particularly, Polar Bear.

When, in contrast, Polar Bear was sick, I could not fail to notice he was the exact opposite of this scenario. He did not wish either any attention called to his malaise or, for that matter, any attention, period — even from me. He would suffer it, the attention, not the sickness — he was very manly about the sickness — but that is all he would do. He wanted to be alone and he wanted to be completely alone. Compared to Polar Bear being sick, Greta Garbo was gregariousness itself and J. D. Salinger a publicity hound.

Needless to say, from the beginning, I could not abide this attitude of his. His wanting to be by himself conjured up in my mind all sorts of stories of elephant graveyards and animals wandering off to die alone. I became indeed so hypochondriacal about it that I was always and invariably certain that whatever it was he had would undoubtedly prove fatal unless I did something about it and did it right away.

More often than not, after either a visit or a call to the vet, such action on my part involved, on his part, a pill. This was not good news. Indeed it was such bad news that I really should change a preceding paragraph about his attitude toward attention. Kindly amend this paragraph to the next to last thing he wanted when he was sick was attention — the very last thing he wanted was a pill. When it came to pills, Polar Bear was not only a Christian Scientist, he wrote the book — and I say this without prejudice because I happen to be a very large admirer of their beliefs.

In any case, I remember well the first time I ever gave Polar Bear a pill. It was late in February, sometime after I had come back from California. As is my wont in such matters, before embarking on such a major enterprise as giving him a pill, I had decided, rather than embarrass myself with Dr. Thompson, I would consult other authorities on this subject. To my surprise, I discovered that there were many articles on either the general or specific topic. The fact that there were so many, I recognized, was hardly a good sign. But I tackled them anyway.

My favorite was an article by Susan Easterly entitled "How to Pill Your Cat." The reason this was my favorite was that Ms. Easterly seemed to address her work to those of us who had, as she put it, a cat of "the independent type" — one whom she identified as one "not prone to doing what you would like him to do."

That certainly, I thought, was Polar Bear. Indeed, he was so far from being "prone" to doing what I would like him to do in such a situation as being pilled that I decided the article could indeed have been written just for him. Without further ado I seized it eagerly.

"First of all," Ms. Easterly wrote, "do not advance upon your cat with feelings of abject terror. Think positively and have the pill ready."

Those were fighting words, and my thoughts harkened back to my Boston ancestor Colonel William Prescott and the Battle of Bunker Hill. If there was one thing I was determined I would not show, it would be terror, and certainly not "abject" terror. Polar Bear would never, I resolved, no matter how difficult the operation to come, see the whites of my eyes. As for thinking positively, my thoughts that first time I advanced on Polar Bear were so positive that I really felt, at that moment, I could have pilled a leopard. And my pill, though well hidden in the palm of my left hand, secured by my fourth finger — so that he would see the rest of my fingers normally extended — was just where I wanted it.

The trouble was that Polar Bear had apparently thoughts which were far from positive. They were, in fact, so negative that I was convinced that he had, by some dastardly subterfuge, where my positives were concerned, broken the code. Indeed, as I advanced on him he seemed to know that not only was I up to something but also that whatever this something was, it was not something he wanted to have anything to do with. And furthermore, some way, somehow, he knew about the pill. As he retreated as negatively as I positively advanced, there was no mistaking the fact that his eyes were riveted on what I thought I had so deftly hidden.

At this juncture I decided that not to advance farther was definitely the better part of valor. Rather I felt I should just hold the line at the ground I had already taken, and dig in. Meanwhile, I turned again to Ms. Easterly. I was sure she would have wise counsel for this kind of stalemate. And I was right. The only trouble was her advice was all too reminiscent of the advice I had received from another source, as all those of you with good memories will recall, about my cat's bath.

"Wrap your cat in a large towel," Ms. Easterly had written, "leaving only the head exposed. This prevents loss of your blood due to flailing claws." I was fully prepared to give blood in reasonable amounts, but I was by no means big on wrapping Polar Bear in a towel. And, I soon learned, after cornering him, neither was he. Nonetheless, I had vowed to follow Ms. Easterly's advice to the letter, and I proceeded to do so.

"Hold the cat firmly against you," Ms. Easterly's advice continued, "in the crook of your arm and on your lap. This allows both your hands to remain free."

Since one of my hands was limited by my arm crook, and the other one by the pill, they were hardly free, but I did my best. And I'm sure Ms. Easterly's advice worked like a charm with her cat — albeit I could not help suspecting that her cat must have been very small, very old, and very sick, if indeed alive at all, when she performed this maneuver. Or that perhaps she has a black belt in karate. In any case, her suggestion did not work with Polar Bear. He shot out of the towel like a dart out of a blowgun.

I am, however, no quitter. I caught him and recovered him — literally in fact with the towel — and this time, instead of my first gentle crook of the arm I held him in such a viselike grip that I elicited from him one of the most baleful "Aeiou" 's I had ever heard. I pretended, of course, that I hadn't heard it, meanwhile reading on by holding the article with my half-free pill hand.

"Place your hand over the cat's head," Ms. Easterly stalwartly continued, apparently at this time engaging a third hand, "using the thumb or forefinger, whichever is preferred, to grasp each corner of the cat's jaw. Apply slight pressure and its mouth will open."

Once more I took Ms. Easterly at her word as best I could, using the crook arm hand. I applied first, as she had suggested, slight pressure. Then I applied slightly more pressure. And finally I applied enough pressure to open the mouth of a crocodile.

The problem was that the mouth did not open. It did not open as much as a single solitary slit. Reluctantly I decided to modify Ms. Easterly's instructions. I took my index finger and, using it like an awl, worked my way into Polar Bear's mouth, a little back of his teeth. At last I had my whole finger in and across his mouth — like a bit in the mouth of a horse. And of course Polar Bear did just what a horse would do — he bit on the bit.

Go ahead, I told him, bite the hand that feeds you, the hand that's doing all this for your own good. He literally gagged on this line but I would not stop. Instead, at his very next gag, I used the opportunity to pop the pill into the back of his mouth.

"Close his mouth immediately," my instructions read, "stroke his throat and the natural reflex action will leave no doubt that the pill has been swallowed. Done properly and quickly, your cat will not even realize that he has ingested a pill."

I did the stroking perfectly. And then, just as I was congratulating myself on a masterful job masterfully performed, something hit me right between the eyes. Well, not exactly between the eyes but in fact on the nose — and it plopped from there to the floor.

It was, of course, the pill. Maybe some cats would not "even realize," as Ms. Easterly had put it, that they had "ingested a pill," but Polar Bear was not of their number. As a matter of fact he had, after firing his bull's-eye, once more jumped out of the towel to the floor and was quietly lying down licking his fancied wounds. From time to time, however, he would fix a by now extremely beady eye on me with just one obvious question on his mind. Would I, or would I not, be foolish enough to answer the bell for the next round? I stared right back at him. What did he think I was made of? Was his memory so short that it could not retain any of the saga of my past triumphs over his intransigence?

I took a deep breath and once more stood up. This time, almost in one masterful maneuver, I grabbed him, wrapped him in the towel, sawed open his mouth, and plopped in the pill. And this time also, after politely telling him to shut his mouth, then, with my hand, actually shutting it, I stroked his throat over and over until I was certain there was not the slightest possibility that he hadn't swallowed it. To make absolutely certain, however, I opened his mouth again, this time with surprising little resistance, I was pleased to note, and peered around inside. No pill anywhere.

I watched him as he went away to lick not only his fancied wounds but also, now, his pride. But I was a gracious winner. I went over, got down on my knees and scrubbed his ears and stomach. "You see, Polar Bear," I told him, "that wasn't so bad after all, was it?" I also told him he couldn't possibly have even tasted the pill. And surely he must realize that he couldn't set himself up as judge and jury of what was best for him. Only I, and his vet, could do that.

As gracious a winner as I was, Polar Bear was, I was glad to see, a gracious loser. I was thinking about this when, out of the corner of my eye, I spotted a telltale white object on the rug behind him. No, I thought, it couldn't be. But of course it was. It was the pill.

For a long moment I said nothing. I just looked at the pill and then, slowly, back at him. Finally he too looked at the pill and then, equally slowly, back at me. There was no doubt about what he was doing — he was smiling.

I rose to my feet with as much of what dignity I had left as I could muster. All right, I thought, if all-out war was what he wanted, all-out war was what he would get. But, I warned him — and he could go to the bank on what I was saying — the next attack would come when he least expected it. I would bide my time and then I would go all out.

And I did just that. I bode in fact for a good long time, because I had made up my mind that a nighttime excursion, under cover of darkness, was my best chance for success. And that night, after he had jumped up on the bed and was fast asleep — using, as usual, about three-quarters of my king-sized bed — I struck. With one single but incredibly rapid motion — one which would have done credit to the late George Patton — I sat up, seized him, plunged the pill into his mouth, and this time not only stroked his throat but, as I did so, all but did the swallowing for him. It was not pretty, but war never is.

The point is that he did indeed that night swallow a pill. But to say he was furious is putting it mildly. If cats can be livid, livid he was. He obviously considered my actions as the greatest doublecross since Brutus stabbed

Caesar. And to his way of thinking, even that dark deed, dastardly as it was, happened after all in broad daylight. What I had done to him had been done in the depths of the night.

Just the same, hard as it was to bear his wrath, the fact remained, from that day to this, or rather from that night to this, that is the way, with slight variations — as, for example, when he is sound asleep in the daytime — that I have administered all pills to him. Let sleeping dogs lie, they say. But where does it say that about sleeping cats?

Hard on the heels of our pill crisis, I was off for Canada and the painting of the seals. We had gotten the good ship *Sea Shepherd* in England and I was to join it in Boston.

Paul had no ship's cat aboard — he had kept that berth open for Polar Bear — but although I did not take him, I thought of him many times on that long and incredibly difficult voyage. Day after day and night after night we would shove ahead at the ice, stop, reverse our engines, go back fifty yards and then smash again — sometimes even riding up on the ice and then crunching down to clear water.

The low point was the fifth night — the night after the seal hunt had started — when a terrific storm had come up and we were icebound. That night I had lain down with my clothes still on, as totally discouraged as we were totally stuck. I must have dozed off when I felt a tugging at my coat. It was Tony, the second mate, a man who had volunteered to join the crew only two days before we had sailed from Boston. "The fog has broken," he said, "and the ship's sprung loose. I think we can make it."

I went up on the bridge with him and looked around. There was no more storm, no more fog, and ahead not even any more ice. There was a clear path to the seals. It was like a miracle. As full throttle we forged ahead I again thought of Polar Bear. He had indeed brought the Fund luck.

A little after midnight, we heard, for the first time, the barking of the seals. Then, suddenly, we saw one. Then another. And another. And another, until there were literally hundreds. On one side of the ship, they had all been clubbed and skinned. On the other, though, they were still untouched. Ahead the lights of the sealing ships were clearly visible, but their crews and clubbers were all apparently fast asleep, preparatory to resuming the next deadly clubbing.

They would have a rude awakening. First Tony stopped the *Sea Shepherd* exactly half a nautical mile away from the seals. I did not want the ship itself arrested, and Canada's so-called "Seal Protection" Act had decreed that nothing, ship or person, could come within half a nautical mile of the sealhunt unless engaged in the killing. It was surely remarkable seal protection.

Nonetheless, one by one, over the side, with their canisters of dye, went our brave, trained, and hand-picked ice crew: Watson, Matt Herron, Joe Goodwin, David Mac-Kinney, Keith Kreuger, Mark Sterck, Eddie Smith, and Paul Pezwick. The Minister of Fisheries had assured the Canadian parliament that the *Sea Shepherd* would never get near enough the seals to see one, let alone paint one. Yet by the next morning we had painted, literally under the seal killers' noses, more than a thousand.

Today, looking back on the event, I realize that our painting of the seals was only one battle in the long war — but it was a victory and it came at a time when a victory was important. The most important battle would not come until four years later — the direct result of the brilliant strategy which was formulated and led by Brian Davies of the International Fund for Animal Welfare. It was Davies who persuaded me that the way to stop commercial sealing was to forget Canada, which was a lost cause anyway, and to concentrate instead on the European Economic Community — the countries which bought the pelts — and get these countries to ban the importation of the baby sealskin into Western Europe. And when this finally came about, what we all liked best was that the ban was put into effect under an already existing EEC law — one which banned foreign pornography.

But Canada, typically, did not give up and four years later resumed commercial clubbing, albeit this time limiting themselves to a 57,000 quota and going after just six- to seven-week-old seals, or, as they are called, "beaters." This time the sealers had apparently found a new buyer for their bloody pelts — Japan. Somehow it figured — Canada and Japan allied together, the seal killers and the dolphin killers.

Back at home at last, I found Polar Bear, having been well cared for by Marian, hale and hearty — in fact, too hearty. No matter how you looked at it, or rather at him, there was no gainsaying the fact that he was — and far too rapidly — gaining weight.

There is a canard about neutered and spayed cats, as there is about neutered or spayed dogs. And this is that they will, after the operation, invariably and almost immediately gain weight. It is not, of course, true. Cats and dogs gain weight from just one thing, and that is that they are eating too much.

At the same time, it is true that animals who were

former strays will often overeat. This could hardly be otherwise because, having gone through periods of intense hunger, they naturally have a tendency to regard each meal as possibly their last. Certainly Polar Bear fell into this category. On the other hand, he did not unfortunately fall into the category of the kind of cat for whom food can be left down in large portions and who can be left to eat whenever they wish to do so and never apparently eat too much. Polar Bear regarded any dish left out, no matter how much was in it, as something to be devoured there and then and that was that.

As if this was not enough, from the very beginning when I had just rescued him, he embarked on a devious and steady campaign of getting people, by hook or by crook, to refill his dish. After, for example, I had fed him his breakfast and had left for the office, he would wait until Rosa, the cleaning lady, would appear. Then, not all the time, because he was too clever for that, but nonetheless most of the time, he would entice Rosa to his by now thoroughly empty bowl — he made sure there was not a trace of food in it — and then, looking up at her, he would emit the most piteous of his remarkable repertoire of piteous "aeiou"'s. At which, of course, Rosa would invariably look at him and his empty bowl and, in a tone of great solicitude, attempt in Spanish to comfort him. "*Pobre gatocito,*" she would croon. "*El señor no te dió desayuno?*" Whereupon, I was sure, Polar Bear would reply, "*No, él no me lo dió.*" When it came to food, I knew he wouldn't let a little thing like a language barrier stand in his way. In any case, Rosa would invariably assure him, "*Pobre Oso Polar, yo te lo voy a dar!*" and promptly fill his bowl to the brim. Thus, having finished Meal No. 1 less than an hour before, Pobre Oso Polar would now tuck into Meal No. 2.

In the late afternoon Marian would arrive, and she too would be greeted by a pathetic and forlorn-looking feline crouched beside an empty bowl. "Precious!" Marian would exclaim. "Didn't Rosa give you anything to eat?" No, not a nibble, Polar Bear, lying in his teeth, would reply — whereupon he would soon be attacking Meal No. 3.

Finally, when I came home, and he well recognized that I was a far tougher nut to crack and that for me neither of his previous performances would suffice, he would let out all the stops. No more would he try the beside-the-empty-bowl crouch, or the piteous "aeiou." Rather, I'd be on the receiving end of a full Broadway-style show — one that began with him flouncing around near the kitchen (but not so obvious as to be actually in it) all the time emitting not loud "aeiou"'s but rather the silent, heart-rending variety immortalized in Paul Gallico's *Silent Miaow*. If he failed to achieve the desired results with these — which, because of my innate suspicions, was often the case — they would be followed by what I can only describe as truly tragic Grand Opera yowls — delivered full throat, head thrown back, chest extended and voice aimed, in the finest operatic tradition, at the very last seat in the very last row of the fifth balcony.

When even this did not work, he would have still one last card to play. This was a series of unspoken but nonetheless clearly visible communications which were invariably accusatory in nature. An example was his all-purpose "If-you-don't-care-neither-do-I"; another was the more specific "If-your-imagination-is-so-limited-that-you-can't-even-picture-what-it-was-like-for-me-when-I-was-hungry-all-the-time" routine. Make no mistake, these were extremely difficult to resist, and, since I really couldn't be sure Rosa and Marian had fed him — something I think he well knew — all too often I also would bow to his multi-faceted manipulations. And that, of course, would be Meal No. 4. Finally, last but not least, would come that late late snack to which I have already alluded and which thus became Meal No. 5.

Looking at him, I realized I would have to call a halt to all this, and I would have to call it immediately. On one memorable Saturday morning, I began. First I took him to the window and held him up so that he could look down at all the people in the park, an extraordinary number of whom were either running, jogging, race walking, or just plain walking. I asked him if he knew what they were doing. He obviously did not because as I could see from the direction of his head he was not paying any attention to them. Instead his eyes were riveted, as they usually are when he is by the window, on pigeons.

I was annoyed at this. I told him that I was fully aware that he was interested in ornithology and in fact was an inveterate bird-watcher or, as the purists had it, birder. But could he not just once, I importuned, direct his attention away from the birds and toward the people? He could not. Finally, I literally had to turn his head. What did he think those people were doing? I asked him again. Did he think they were running or jogging or race walking or walking just for the fun of it? Of course not, I answered myself. What they were doing was keeping in shape.

When he would again be distracted by the pigeons, I would remind him that I had no doubt that even some of them had succumbed to the trend. In any case, I was warming to my task. Why, I went on, did he think there was so much calorie counting nowadays? So many no-cal drinks. So many sugar substitutes. The whole world, I told him sternly, was on a fitness kick. And, I assured him, it wasn't just a fitness kick for people, either. Animals too were involved in it. And not just the pigeons — cats too, I said, were. I always like to bring things home to him.

Furthermore, I went on, the idea of the whole thing was not just to be more attractive to the opposite sex— I did not want to dwell on that in view of his recent operation, and all — it was also, and far more importantly, due to a desire to be, just for oneself, healthier and more fit and to live a longer, fuller, and happier life. I was reaching my peroration now, and I began to raise my voice. Even if he understood nothing else, I stated firmly, I wanted him to get one thing straight — that Thin Was In and Fat Was Out. With this I actually turned his head back toward me and this time did shout a question at him — Did He Or Did He Not Want To Be The Last Fat Cat In The World?

He did not answer — something which I could easily have put down to the fact that he does not like loud talk, particularly when it involved personal criticism. I did not allow myself to dwell on this, however. Instead I decided to take his refusal to answer as a sign that no, he did not want to be the last fat cat in the world. Well, then, I concluded as cheerfully as I could, there were just no two ways about it — he would have to go on a diet. And, so that there could be no possible doubt in his mind, I repeated this. Diet, I said, diet.

I knew from the beginning, of course, that he would think very little of the idea. But I was determined. There would be no more badgering of Rosa and Marian and cadging of extra meals from them. Nor would there be any more heaping dishfuls — there would be smaller portions and they would occur at lengthier intervals. I also pursued what I thought were two excellent lines of approach to overcome whatever objections he might have. First, I reminded him, there was nothing to be ashamed of. He was not being singled out. Everyone, people and cats, was inclined to put on a few extra pounds as he or she got older — or rather, more mature. Second, I told him, even I myself had occasionally considered going on a diet. I knew he could certainly identify with this and I went to some lengths to tell him a story that had almost persuaded me in the dietary direction.

It had happened, I told him, only a few months before he came, when I had had occasion to visit a New York men's store — one in which, when the spirit, or rather Marian, moved me, I sometimes bought a new suit. The store was called Imperial Wear, I informed him, and it advertised itself as carrying clothes for the "Big and Tall." One day, however, I had had a nasty experience there. I happened to arrive at the store when my regular salesman was otherwise occupied, and I unluckily received a rank newcomer who stupidly took me to a section which I clearly saw was marked "Portly."

I was furious, of course. I am not fond of the word *portly* — in fact it is one of the very few old-fashioned words which I do not like — and in no uncertain terms I made my feelings clear to the young whippersnapper. Whereupon he nervously and rapidly informed me that the store used the word only for the style of the suit, and that actually "portly" was for thinner people than, for example, another of the sections, which he pointed out, was called, bluntly, "Stout."

I told Polar Bear that of course that made me feel a great deal better, and I actually even "My good manned" the young man a few times while he went on to explain that even the "Stouts" were divided into the "Long Stouts" and the "Stylish Stouts." But just the same the whole thing was, when you got right down to it, a close call. In fact, I told Polar Bear, I had not gone on a diet on that occasion but on the occasion of his diet, I would do so. In a sense, indeed, I explained to him, we would both be going on a diet together. I would do all the difficult part — the research, and the counting of calories and all that sort of thing — and all he would have to do would really be the minor part — after all my work was done — of just the not eating. I emphasized that I had always been a great believer in the idea of diets — the only trouble was that I had found, through experience, that I was much better at reading about them than I was at not eating them.

From that Saturday on I felt that at least we had come to some sort of understanding about the whole matter. I immediately cut down his portions and demanded that Rosa, on pain of never again being allowed to feed him, even when I was there, stop giving in to his performances. With Marian I had more difficulty. Marian is very bad at taking direct orders anyway, and, despite my remonstrances, was always giving him, as she put it, "just a tad more." In desperation I told her that she would either cease and desist or the next time I was at her apartment I would do something she never does — which is cut her cat's toenails. That did it.

Unfortunately it didn't do it for Polar Bear's diet. Smaller portions or no smaller portions, it was soon apparent that we were not only not winning the diet war, we were losing it. Polar Bear was still merrily gaining away as if there was no tomorrow — which, I stonily reminded him, there might well not be if he refused to buckle down. I would have to take more drastic steps.

What I decided upon this time was to put him on special food — diet cat food. Here the battle was joined with the very first can. Polar Bear did not like the look of it from the moment he saw me opening it. This was no fault of the food people. Polar Bear, as I have said, does not like anything new, and if there is one thing new which he especially does not like, it is new food.

I had purposely decided to try it on him on a weekend when I could be there all the time, and I was very glad of my decision that first Saturday morning when I put down the first bowl of it and saw he would not touch it, even though I knew full well he was hungry. All right, I thought sternly, if he wanted to play hardball I could play hardball too, and I promptly took it away. But I told him that when I was a small boy I had to eat everything on my plate or otherwise what I had left would be brought back again cold before the next meal and that if I didn't eat that first there would be no next meal. A great many Boston boys, I told him, had been brought up that way and they were all the better for it. In those days it was called "making a Hoover plate" — in honor of Herbert Hoover's relief program for the Belgian children. And although I didn't expect him to remember that, he could jolly well learn the same lesson because that was the way I intended to handle him.

Saturday noon I brought out the same dish again. Again, nothing. Once more I took it away. And, once more, I waited. This time I waited through an entire afternoon of caterwaulings. I ignored them. This was Valley Forge.

At dinnertime when, for the third time, I repeated the process and when, also for the third time, he stonewalled me, this time, before taking the dish away, in desperation and right in front of him, I put a finger in the food, licked it, and beamed at him. "Mmmmm," I said, "delicious." He watched me intently, but with an expression on his face of a medieval potentate watching a taster whom he had reason to suspect bite into a dish which he had purposely laced with poison.

I ignored the look and persisted. Even for his late night snack I brought back the diet food and told him it would be that or nothing. Again, nothing it was. And that night I underwent a steady rolling barrage of "aeiou" 's. Then, when I had finally managed despite these to drop off to sleep he promptly proceeded to flounce around on the bed until he was able to wake me again — a condition he had obviously calculated would bring me to my senses.

By the next morning when he had been twenty-four straight hours without food — and yet still refused so much as a morsel — I was frankly worried. But I knew I had only two alternatives — either bravely to stay the course or cravenly to give in to his blackmail. It was a measure of my mettle that, damning the torpedoes, I boldly marched to the icebox. This time, however, as I took down the same dish, before I even had a chance to put it down in front of him, he uttered a truly piercing "aeiou". And right here I want to make something perfectly clear about our battle — and that is that I did not give in, and he did not win. What happened was that, when he uttered that "aeiou," I happened to look carefully at that dish and I decided that it really might be spoiled or something and that if I made him eat it, it actually might make him sick. That and that only was the reason not to give him any more diet food but to go back to his regular food. But to say that he won, or indeed to place any other such interpretation on my action, is simply unwarranted by the facts. And, of course, it should be remembered that it was I, not Polar Bear, who made the decision.

I did so, as always, for a very good reason. This was because I had decided that, in the whole broad picture of any fitness program — I am very good at broad pictures — diet is only, when you come right down to it, a part of it. Equally important is exercise. A diet without exercise, I have always said, is only half a diet. I, for example, not only occasionally cut down on desserts but at the same time every weekend when the weather is clement, take out my bicycle and have a good hard ride. It takes me almost ten minutes to reach the chess tables in the middle of Central Park and, after a few hours there, I take a good brisk ride home. I credit this program not with any such nonsense as being able to get into my old army uniform — frankly, I think that is a ridiculous ambition — but with keeping me, both physically and mentally, in top shape.

For contrast, Polar Bear was, I realized, just lying around far too much of the time. And since he would obviously not do anything about this, it was equally obviously up to me. He was not fond of chess, and so I developed for him a wide variety of other games. In the living room I would first get out all his balls and any other toys which would roll and, one by one, I would entice him into, if not actually retrieving them — that would have been for him too demeaningly doglike — at least going after them on the double. Then, in the bedroom at night before going to sleep, I would stuff him under a thin blanket or sheet and begin a series of slow-starting but fast-ending finger pokes. My favorite was one that started from behind him where he couldn't see it and ended right smack in the pit of his ample stomach. Whereupon he would then have a fair go, with all four paws and a bite to boot, at the offending digit. After this, it was understood that it was his turn to go on the offensive, and he would come out from under the blanket or sheet with fire in his eye and mayhem on his mind. I would meet his charge and this time we would really go to the mat and have a wrestling match — one which would put to shame those shams you see on television. Even when I finally got him down, he would not give up. Instead, he would just pretend to do so, hoping that I would, for a second, relax my hold. And, when I inevitably did so, it was San Juan Hill all over again. If his front paws, or rather claws, didn't suffice to do the job, he would call in the reserves. These were of course his back claws. And these, with his back legs used as battering rams and the claws as rotating rakes, were extraordinarily effective.

Finally, after a definite "uncle" had been cried, usually by me, and all falls and points tallied, he would jump up and take a victory lap — actually a victory leap — around the whole apartment. All in all, for him it was a pretty fair workout and was at least more successful in the fitness department than any of the diet experiments. For me, however, as the blood on my fingers and hands clearly attested, it was no walk in the Park. And one night, as I was watching his victory lap and was in fact actually thinking of the expression I had used for what it had all been for me, I realized that I had, inadvertently, thought of exactly what he did need — a walk in the Park.

Indoor exercise, fine as it was, was simply not enough. All Bostonians worthy of the name have always put a good deal of stock into taking good, old-fashioned walks or, as in happier times they were called, constitutionals — and I was no exception. All right, cats were not dogs, but it was nonsense, I decided, to say that you could not walk a cat. You could walk anything if the will was there, and the discipline, and you had that rare combination of know-how and stick-to-it-iveness which had ever been my hallmark in my relations with Polar Bear.

I did my usual faithful research, and, in short order, I put Operation Catwalk on my front burner. First, I procured a harness and then after doing my best to make it fit and get Polar Bear into it — neither of which was as easy as it sounds — I then turned to making a game out of the whole thing so that I could get him, if not to make friends with his new harness, at least to make a semblance of peace with the idea of being in it.

At last I was ready for in-house practice. I stood with the leash with plenty of play in it, as instructed, and waited patiently for him to decide where he wanted to go. Unfortunately, he didn't want to go anywhere. He just crouched and, with his tail moving ominously, looked at me. The look clearly said, "So now I'm going to live in a straitjacket?" I told him that this question was undeserving of a serious answer. He was, as usual, making a mountain out of a molehill — he could go anywhere his little heart desired. With that I gave the leash even more play, in the hopes that he would at least do me the courtesy of taking a step or two. But it was no dice. Finally, I myself made just the hint of a move in his favorite direction, at the same time quietly asking him if he wanted to go into the kitchen.

The moment that word *kitchen* was out of my mouth, he leapt. The next thing I knew he was in there, aeiouing, of course, for lunch — without me, without leash, and without harness. He had somehow gathered up both front and back legs at once and jumped through, under, or over it.

Now there was nothing to do but give him a snack — something which was, after all, hardly the idea of the entire program. And then, following this, for me and for the harness, it was back to the drawing board.

Finally I had that harness so that Houdini couldn't have gotten out of it. But, once more, I was just standing there and he was not moving. Indeed in all our in-house practice he moved only twice, once when the telephone rang — he likes it to stop ringing as soon as possible — and the other time when the doorbell rang and a chess player appeared. At this I decided to suspend our training exercises.

After the chess player had gone, I also decided that perhaps any more in-house practice was really a waste of time. There wasn't any real reason for him to move around inside anyway — it was time to move out.

I picked him up and carried him to the elevator. There was a woman going down and, as I put him down, she was very interested. "Oh," she said, "you're walking him. I didn't know you could, with cats. How on earth did you ever get him to do it?"

Practice, I told her, and persistence — it hadn't been easy. After this, when we reached the ground floor, I was looking forward to an impressive promenade across the lobby. So, of course, Polar Bear stayed in the elevator. And, while we were discussing the matter, the elevator, of course, went up again. This time we went all the way to the penthouse floor, where my rock group friend got on. "That's something," he said. "Walking a cat! I didn't know that could be done." I told him there was really nothing to it, once you got the hang of it. This time, though, once we had reached the ground floor again, I not only picked Polar Bear up, I carried him through the lobby, across the street, and well into Central Park. Then, after a last double-check of the harness, I gingerly set him down.

I must say he was very interested in everything — particularly, in order, the birds, the dogs, and the squirrels, and although I had the distinct impression that he regarded the latter as a very peculiar breed of climbing mouse, at least I felt we had made a start. With all his looking, however, he refused to budge so much as an inch. I waited and waited. He could get this much exercise, I thought, sleeping.

Suddenly, from behind us, I heard a loud woof. I spun around and, coming directly at us at full gallop, was an Afghan — one which, at that moment, looked to me like the largest one I had ever seen. I leapt for Polar Bear and at the same time delivered what I can only describe as the fastest hip check a man my age is capable of administering.

The next moment all three of us, the Afghan, Polar Bear, and I, were on the ground in an assembled heap. As I tried to get up, still shielding Polar Bear, a young lady, leash in hand, came running up. Ignoring me, she went straight for her dog. "Poor Alfie," she cried. Then, after putting the leash on him, and before she had even seen Polar Bear, she whirled on me. "I saw what you did," she said. "You attacked my dog. You ought to be . . ." She stopped because at that moment she had spotted, burrowing into my shoulder, a hissing Polar Bear. "Oh," she said, "a cat! Alfie hates cats!" I attempted to point out that, as she could surely see, Polar Bear wasn't all that fond of Afghans, either. The young lady ignored this and proceeded to deliver a stern lecture about the idiocy of trying to walk a cat anywhere, and particularly in Central Park. I protested that at least he had been on a leash and that, as Alfie had, after all, been off his, it seemed to me that I was hardly the only one at fault. I soon realized, however, that I was getting nowhere on that tack, and so I finally gave up, telling her merely that I would admit to the illegal block and would gladly accept a fifteen-yard penalty. With that, and with as much aplomb as I could muster, I moved off — hopefully to pastures new.

I went, as a matter of fact, quite some little distance, hoping that Polar Bear might, in the meantime, calm down. And this time I chose an area which I had thoroughly cased and determined to be one hundred percent dog-free. Then, and only then, did I once more lower Polar Bear to the ground.

And once more I waited — so interminably in fact that I was half asleep when, like a shot, Polar Bear bolted. And he bolted so fast and so unexpectedly that he took the leash right out of my hand. Frozen, I watched him fly over the grass after a squirrel. When I finally started after him, I was already so far behind that I could barely see the squirrel tear up a tree and, worse, see Polar Bear tear right up after him, his leash bouncing along behind him. Obviously it would catch on a knob or a small branch or something, and he would hang to death right over my head.

Amazingly, the leash did not catch — only because, by luck, the squirrel had quickly turned off to a branch and Polar Bear's leash was now not trailing behind him, it was hanging down. But the branch which the squirrel had chosen, though long, would in time become reed-thin. And, even if it could have held the squirrel, it could certainly not have held Polar Bear.

Whatever was going to happen, I realized, was better than hanging, but at the same time he was bound sooner or later to fall — and from a dangerous height. As I watched, the squirrel disappeared. For a moment I thought he might have leapt to another branch, but he had not. Instead, he had turned and run back underneath the branch. And, just when the squirrel ran under him, Polar Bear whirled.

He did not touch the squirrel, but he lost touch with the branch and lost his balance. As he fell, I jumped forward. Although I have always fancied myself as one of the greatest wide receivers ever to be overlooked by the Harvard team, I would have to admit that in this instance it was by pure luck rather than sheer skill that I caught him.

Sinking to my knees for a long moment, I just hugged him to my stomach. Then softly I spoke to him, I told him it was time to go home now. He obviously agreed and, as I carried him home, although I was prepared to admit we had probably had both our first and our last walk on a leash, I would still not admit it was any fault of mine, or, for that matter, his. It was simply because of forces beyond the control of either of us. It was, in truth, a jungle out there.

All right, the carpers and the nay-sayers could argue that up to now my diet programs and my exercise endeavors had not been howling successes. But, as I believe I have told you before and probably will again, I am no easy giver-upper or giver-inner. Long before Vince Lombardi or whoever it was said, "When the going gets tough, the tough get going," or Yogi Berra said, "It's never over till it's over," it should be remembered that I was saying, "If you can't play a sport, be one."

And the fact was, win, lose, or draw, I was determined to be a sport to the end about Polar Bear's fitness program. But I was also just as determined, for the good of his little soul as much as mine, to have some kind of clear-cut victory. So far, however, just how to accomplish this had eluded me. But one warm spring day, standing on my balcony, I had a brainstorm.

I have these brainstorms, if I do say so, with some regularity. But this particular one was special. I had gone out, as is my wont, to regard the world. And that lovely evening, as I was enjoying the scenery, it suddenly occurred to me that here I was, seeing all the sights in the street below and the Park beyond, and yet Polar Bear could not do this. He had to see it all from behind a window, which was not the same thing at all. It was wrong — he should be enjoying it just as I was.

But how, I thought — I'm very logical in my brainstorms — could he possibly do this? The only way would be to wire in the whole balcony. And the only way that could be accomplished would, even if the building were to allow it, only be unsightly from their point of view, but from mine it would ruin my actual view.

Your average inventor might have given up right then and there. But I was hardly your average inventor. When I am working on an invention I break it down step by step, as all the great inventors of the past have done. If you do not do this, you end with a stumbling block and your whole thing is half-baked.

As I thought of that, the answer came. There was no

need to wire in all the balcony — all that had to be done was just to wire in half the balcony. It was the perfect solution. But there was, still, one more step to overcome. There was only one door. If half of the balcony, unwired, included the door for me to get in and out, how would he get in and out of his wired half?

Again, this might have stopped your average inventor in his tracks. But it did not stop yours truly. Instead, I decided on a careful inspection of the site — always a crucial part of any great innovative idea. And, as I looked, once more the solution came — he could get in and out to his half from the bedroom window.

And so, step by step, I had climbed every mountain. There just remained the minor detail of getting the proper help for the job. A great inventor I might be and a great engineer as well — even, perhaps, a great architect, although up to this time I had never actually entered that field — but one thing I am not. And that is, as I have mentioned before, a great builder. Nor am I, if the truth be known, a great spender — in fact I have been called, I think much too loosely, the last of the small spenders. But I was certainly not about to go out and spend a small fortune for wirers, roofers, and heaven knows what else for what? For just a simple little job like that.

No indeed I was not, thank you very much. And, by pure chance, the very next afternoon a locksmith was coming to my apartment to install what a friend had recommended — a burglarproof lock.

Watching the man work, I started complimenting him. Not so lavishly, of course, as to be obvious. I simply told him that he was a fine worker and that a man with his talent must be able to fix or even build just about anything.

But did he not, I asked, sometimes get tired of working only on locks?

The man looked up at me expectantly. I pulled back. I told him it was nothing, I was just thinking of a tiny little job I had — one that was hardly worthy of his talents. There was more talk, of course, but the long and short of it was — the short being that, like all New York workmen, he charged me an arm and a leg. Nonetheless, the next morning, actually on time, the man arrived. With him he had yards of chicken wire, wood, bolts, and a wide variety of tools. And, by the following day, Polar Bear had his balcony.

Spring or no spring, that night, as it happened, snow fell. It was one of those rare but heavy snowfalls which sometimes blanket the city in late March. I realized, of course, I would have to postpone the christening of the balcony — there were at least five inches of snow — but Polar Bear would have none of it. He stood on the windowsill and practically banged his head against the glass to have it opened. In vain I remonstrated with him. He would not want to go out there now, I told him.

My arguments were useless — and so, as usual, I gave in. I opened the window and out he jumped. As he sank into the snow up to his stomach, he froze and made no attempt to move. Then, slowly, he swiveled his head and looked at me. "Well," the look clearly said, "you surely bleeped it up this time!"

Actually I took it as a compliment — obviously he now felt that I, at master control, was responsible for everything, even the weather outside. And as time went on and the weather improved, the balcony not only served him well — he could, in perfect safety, crouch down and lash around and be a big shot with the pigeons — it also, surprisingly enough, pleased the pigeons. Soon learning that he could not actually get at them, they in turn became big shots too. They cooed and chirruped at him to their hearts' content, ruffled their feathers within his vision, and promenaded boldly across his roof.

Besides this the balcony proved itself such an attraction that, in showing it off, I was able to expound on one of my many pet cat theories. This one concerned people who live in the country and regularly allow their cats to go out — often either at fatal peril from dogs or automobiles, to them, or at peril to the surrounding birds from them. Polar Bear or no Polar Bear, I feel that no cat owner has the right to jeopardize the right of his neighbor who may enjoy his birds just as the cat owner enjoys his cat. The ideal solution would seem to be something like my balcony — a good-sized outdoor, wired-in walk, one which could end, say, at a cat door at the kitchen. The cat could then go out whenever he wished — but he would be safe and so too would the birds.

I am very firm about this theory — so firm that I have actually dreamed of taking out a patent on it. I even dream of sitting back and watching such catwalks going up all over the country — with, of course, just a reasonable little royalty being divided, say, like the balcony itself, half to Polar Bear and half to me.

IX ∘ *His Foreign Policy*

Polar Bear's foreign policy, like that of some of our Presidents, left a good deal to be desired. On the domestic front, as we have seen, he had his ups and downs, but even when he was having the latter — when he was, so to speak, taking his lumps — he took them well. He was not the world's brightest cat, but he had unfailing charm and he was a great little communicator — not only with his tail but also with his grin, which was compounded of about equal parts of Morris, Garfield, and pure Cheshire.

When it came to his conduct of foreign affairs, however, the very qualities which had stood him in such good stead and had served so well domestically seemed here to fail him utterly. Again, like some of our Presidents, it was not that he did not like the idea of handling his own foreign policy — he did. Rather it was that he liked it too much and would not entrust it to people who knew far more than he did about the intricacies and nuances of it. And therein lay all the trouble. Because foreign policy is, when you get right down to it, something you either have a feel for, or something you do not. And, bluntly, Polar Bear did not. For one thing, diplomacy — the art of playing up to others and, even when you don't like them, never letting them know it — which is, in sum, the key to foreign policy, bored him. He was always going around it, or under it, or ignoring it altogether. For another thing, on the personal level, on which he was so effective domestically, no one, friend or foe, ever really knew where they stood with him. At times, particularly with small adversaries, he was the Rambo of the cat world and therefore seemed a bully, which he really was not. At other times, particularly with larger adversaries, although he spoke loudly and carried a very large stick — his tail really is enormous — he sometimes seemed nothing more than a feline version of Caspar Milquetoast, which of course he was not either.

But, not to beat about the bush any longer, he was one very prejudiced cat. He was, as a matter of fact, a mass or rather a morass of prejudices. Again, the parallel with certain Presidents comes, perhaps unfairly, to mind. In any case, I do not mean by this that all he cared about were equally fortunate fat cats. And certainly it is not right to say that all he cared about were just other white cats. But whether he would have, were it not for the fact that all cats are supposedly color-blind, is a moot point. In any case, I would not have bet on it, if for no other reason than because he had just about every other prejudice it is possible to have and still, in a changing world, survive.

I shall address first his foreign policy toward other animals. Frankly, it was terrible. Will Rogers once said he never met a man he didn't like — a saying I have always put down to the fact that the late Mr. Rogers must have had a very limited acquaintanceship. But whether he did or not, Polar Bear was assuredly the opposite of Mr. Rogers. I really don't think he ever met another animal he did like.

Some he disliked, it is true, more than others. Some he purely disdained and some he just ignored. In fact about the only animals I believe he didn't feel one of these ways about were horses. He thought they were too big, of course, and made too much noise and he felt that when they went on city streets, for example, they should wear sneakers. But they did not annoy him beyond that and he had basically a live-and-let-live attitude toward them.

It was not so with other animals. Take, for example, his foreign policy toward dogs. To a great many people, dogs are the best-loved animals on earth. Indeed the more fanatical of these people are particularly fond of the old saying that the very word "dog" is God spelled backwards. To Polar Bear, on the other hand, dogs, no matter how you spelled them, were, if not God's greatest mistake — he was not fond of serpents either — then so close to it that the difference was negligible. Furthermore he carried this prejudice against dogs to every single member of the far-flung dog family — even, I am certain, to those I have no evidence he ever met, except rarely, on television, and he did not like them there.

This for me was very bad news, not only because I had, prior to the coming of Polar Bear, always been, as I have already stated, a dog man, but also for another reason. This is that the Fund for Animals, like most organizations of its kind, is often and intimately involved in the rescue of and finding homes for strays. Although about half of these are cats, the fact remained that the other half are dogs. And, when these strays are rescued, in between the time when we pick them up and a permanent home can be found for them, it is often necessary to obtain for them temporary quarters. Thus, almost all of us have, at one time or another, used for this purpose our own abodes.

All in all, it was, therefore, only a matter of time before a stray would find its way to my apartment. While I had a fifty-fifty chance of it being another cat, I also had a fifty-fifty chance of it being a dog. It was, when you came right down to it, a toss of the coin. And, as bad luck would have it, the team Polar Bear lost the toss. The very first stray which appeared that spring was a dog.

The woman who would be bringing it one early Saturday morning had called me first, and she could not have been more apologetic. She knew I had a cat. But, she told me, she simply could not keep the dog she had found the night before even for the rest of the day, and certainly not for the whole weekend. She already had three dogs, and if she took in another she would, she said, be thrown out of her apartment, not only by her superintendent but also by her husband.

I had, of course, no alternative. And the woman was absolutely positive she would have a permanent home for the dog by Monday at the latest. "He's really," she said, "a darling dog."

When she arrived I stepped out to meet her and closed the door behind me. I had already planned my strategy in regard to Polar Bear, and it did not include that his first confrontation with this darling should be in front of this woman. If there were to be casualties, I should be first and darling second — they should not include either Polar Bear or a stranger.

At first look the dog seemed to me, after Polar Bear, the size of a Great Dane. He was not, of course. Unfortunately, however, he was by no means a small dog. Equally unfortunately he was, despite his size, obviously a puppy. And, equally obviously, as close to a totally untrained one as it is possible to imagine. Finally, and perhaps most unfortunately of all, uncertain as was his ancestry, one thing was patently certain about it — he was some kind of retriever mix. While there are in all of dogdom probably no more lovable animals than retrievers, at the same time they are also among the closest things in the animal world to a perpetual motion machine. This was the kind of dog which seems to have no walk — but rather to have just three gaits, run, leap, and bounce. In fact the woman had already named him Bouncer.

Once the woman had unbounced Bouncer and handed me his leash, I opened the door and proceeded to march, or come as close to marching as one could with such an animal, directly to my bedroom. During this march I kept a weather eye out for Polar Bear. I did not see him but I assumed that from wherever he was, he got at least one look.

The moment I closed the bedroom door, Bouncer leapt at it. I ignored this, however, and, after I had gotten him some water, I closed it again and went to see where Polar Bear was. He had repaired, as I might have expected, to the mantelpiece and, having obviously had his look, was on full alert. He was indeed so totally rigid that he looked exactly like one of my animal sculptures up there. It was clear that he was one of the last of the soldiers of Troy and I was the Greek who had brought in the Trojan horse.

Now, Polar, I told him in my best falsely confident voice, we will have none of this. Look at you, I continued. You would think I had brought in the Creature from the Lost Lagoon. Why, it's nothing but a little — I stumbled over that word *little* — friend. A friendly fellow, I added, who had no home. Polar Bear just looked at me, until I amended my explanation. Well, I went on, maybe he was fair-sized, but he was still, I emphasized, a puppy. I was trying desperately to get him to accept any part of my explanation as accurate.

I did not succeed. The thought that enormous as the dog already was, he was going to grow even bigger, obviously did not appeal to Polar Bear. I took another tack. It was not even my fault, somebody else had brought the dog to us — now it was up to both of us to be the hosts. Bouncer was our guest, and surely both of us had merely done what anyone with half a heart would do. We were not, after all, giving up our home, we were merely giving up a part of it — and at that temporarily — to a creature who was in dire need just as, he would surely remember, he had once been.

Polar Bear's answer to this line of argument was to go on the attack himself. He jumped off the mantelpiece and streaked for the bedroom door, where, knowing, of course, that he was perfectly safe, he proceeded to scratch and make warlike "aeiou" 's. This of course so excited Bouncer that he not only scratched back from his side of the door but began to bark loudly.

I sat down. I was well mindful of the fact that new dogs and old cats — or vice versa — should never be put together until they have been properly introduced, and that this should never be done until they have been kept separated at least for long enough to have gotten used to the idea of each other. Maybe, I thought hopefully, this was all part of that idea of getting used to each other. Maybe too, I hoped, the door could stand the gaff.

In any case, I let Polar Bear's scratching and aeiouing and Bouncer's bounding and barking go on as long as I could. Finally, when I could stand it no longer, I went over and picked up Polar Bear and carried him away from the door and into the kitchen. Then, while he was eating, I took the opportunity to prepare a bowl of dog food for Bouncer and take it into the bedroom. I assumed that Polar Bear would be too occupied to notice what I was doing.

I was wrong. He looked up from his food — a very rare thing — and watched me with an expression which made his previous attitude seem friendly. Now, he was saying, I was going to *feed* the monster. In his firm opinion, I had reached the depths of my treachery. I was not just the Greek in Troy, I was Benedict Arnold in Washington's tent.

After Bouncer had eaten, I decided it was time for a walk. Ignoring Polar Bear completely, I marched Bouncer to the door, stopping only to get my bicycle out of the closet, and in short order Bouncer and the bicycle and I were on our way.

Bouncer was surprisingly good on the leash, even beside the bicycle. And, when we arrived at the Park chess tables, although he really didn't sit at all, he was, at least for him, relatively placid while I had my chess game. He was also very popular with some of my chess friends and, by the time I headed home, I felt even more confident about the woman being able to find him a permanent home.

That night I decided it wasn't really fair to leave Polar Bear out there in the living room and have Bouncer with me in the bedroom. And so, carrying Polar Bear high enough to avoid Bouncer's highest bound, I reversed their room reservations. Although it was hardly a restful night — with the endless sniffings and chargings of both parties at the bottom of the door — somehow it was not as bad as I had envisioned it might be. At least it was not so bad that it dissuaded me from putting into operation the next morning my master plan for ending our ridiculous apartment apartheid.

It was to be a face-to-face meeting, and I worked out the details as carefully as if I were arranging a Summit. I did not actually prepare an agenda but I did just about everything else. I decided I would kneel between them at all times, would keep Bouncer on his leash in my right hand, and with my left would have a firm hold on Polar Bear. I would also pay close attention to all noises and, if there was a loud growl from Bouncer or a menacing hiss from Polar Bear, I would abort the mission. At the same time, I would ignore all minor threats and, if I could possibly do so, I would not allow the meeting to break up until there was, if not a lasting peace, at least a temporary Camp David.

I was so proud of the way I had planned it all that, after taking Bouncer for his morning walk, I came in brimming with confidence. I opened the outer door and, instead of turning left to the bedroom, moved briskly into the living room. The moment I missed the turn, of course, Polar Bear leapt to the mantelpiece. I could not allow this deviation from my plan for kneeling between them. And so, with Bouncer on the leash in my right hand, I reached for Polar Bear on the mantelpiece with my left.

I might as well have reached for quicksilver. Still holding Bouncer, I groped and groped. It was no use. I could not touch Polar Bear, let alone grab him. Finally I was reduced to holding the entire meeting in a kind of bent-over-backwards stance, my left hand still groping and my right endeavoring, with the leash, to curb Bouncer's incurable desire to bound himself onto the mantelpiece. To make matters worse, Bouncer could not get a good fix on Polar Bear either. All he saw, all he could be really sure of, with each upward leap, was a constantly batting paw.

All right, I decided, so my Nobel Peace efforts were starting slowly — at least things could not get worse. And, in fact, they did not. I died hard, but after I had been between them for what seemed an hour and had seen not so much as one iota of change in Polar Bear's attitude, I had no alternative but to come to the reluctant conclusion that the chances of Polar Bear's ever recognizing Bouncer's right to anything, even to exist, were extremely nil.

Then, with as much dignity as I could muster, I took Bouncer into the bedroom and shut the door. But this time, instead of going back to stay with Polar Bear, I remained with Bouncer. I was determined to show Polar Bear just what I thought of his rotten foreign policy.

Later that afternoon, after I had taken Bouncer for another walk, I went into the living room to have a talk with Polar Bear. I was hardly pleased with him, but I realized that what had transpired had not, by any means, been entirely his fault. The dog/cat antipathy was deep-rooted, and the dog had, after all, come into Polar Bear's territory. And, when push came to shove — which it surely would — Polar Bear could hardly have been expected to understand that Bouncer's presence was to be only temporary.

As I entered the room, I called cheerfully to him, careful not to use the offensive "Come," merely to request his presence with my usual "Where's Polar Bear?" He did not respond. I called more loudly. Still nothing. I began to look for him. I looked all over the living room. I looked under the sofa and I looked under the desk. I looked in the closets. As I went on looking, the whole thing began to be all too reminiscent of that first night I had him. Which reminded me, of course, to look into the dishwasher. He was not there — he was nowhere.

Well, I thought, he was playing a game. If he was, two could play that game. This time, when I went in the kitchen, I opened the refrigerator door. That would get him, I knew, and on the run.

But the refrigerator door did not get him. I started to look again, and again I looked everywhere. Then, slowly but steadily, I felt a growing alarm. He had gotten out.

But how, I thought, could he? The door had not been opened. Thinking again, however, I realized that it had — it had been opened when I had taken Bouncer for a walk and again when I had brought him home. And both of these times, encumbered as I was with both Bouncer and the bicycle, and not really looking for Polar Bear because I had been so annoyed with him, it might indeed have been possible that he had somehow sneaked out and perhaps flown down the hall. On second thought, that really wouldn't have been possible. Surely I would have seen him.

I called again, loudly, and by now desperately. And this time, as I started to search again, I had still a third thought about his getting out. Either when I was taking Bouncer out or in, it *was* possible.

By now really worried, I went out in the hall. I knew the people in the apartments on my floor knew him but I wondered if he could have gotten off the floor — perhaps through the fire stairs door, when someone had opened it, perhaps through the door to the back elevator. Perhaps indeed he had gotten on the back elevator. Or even on the front elevator, when it had opened to let somebody off. But, I asked myself, wouldn't anybody who got on or off at that floor and seen him get on, have also seen that he was alone and stopped to pick him up, try to find out where he belonged, and bring him back to me?

Of course there was another possibility — a guest or a delivery man. They wouldn't have known where he belonged. They might even have thought he was used to getting on the elevator by himself.

I realized I was rapidly getting so wrought up that I was not thinking clearly. The first thing I would have to do was to stop and decide where, if he had gotten out, he might go. With that in mind, I took the elevator downstairs and told both George, on the front door, and Jimmy on the back, the bad news. Polar Bear, I told them, had gotten loose. Would they be good enough to pass the word?

Everyone was extremely concerned. Raymond, the maintenance man, offered to help me look up on the roof and also down in the basement — two possibilities I had not even, in my distraught state, considered. First we explored the roof. Fortunately, messy as it all was up there, there were not too many hiding places where Polar Bear could have been. But the basement was a different story. I do not know how many non–New York apartment dwellers have ever visited a New York apartment basement, but I assure you that, in even a relatively small building, there are more hiding places for a small animal than it is possible to imagine.

When Raymond and I had searched everywhere we could think of, and I had told everybody I could find of my loss, I went back upstairs and called Marian. She would come over right away.

With Marian I made another search, only this time, after our inside search, we also made an out-of-the-apartment search. I suggested that he might even have run into the Park — after all, he was familiar with it from our ill-fated walk.

We had no luck. Polar Bear was nowhere and night was coming on. Back upstairs we made plans. The next morning we would call all the animal shelters, we would take advertisements in the newspapers, we would place those pathetic "Lost" signs one sees on telephone poles and on trees. As we worked on our plans, I told Marian that I had no one to blame but myself. I had foisted another animal on Polar Bear and I had taken away his sense of security. He thought he was unwanted and he had done the only thing he felt he had to do — run away. He would be killed by a dog, hit by a car, or end up in a laboratory. And it would serve me right, because it had been all my fault. But he would be the one who would do the suffering.

Marian would not allow me to carry on in this vein. "I am still not satisfied," she said, "that he could really have gotten out in the first place. Maybe he's still right here." With that she started once more a search of her own. "Have you looked behind the books?" she asked. I admitted I had not, but I reminded her that Polar Bear was now so big that it would be almost impossible for him to fit back there. Nonetheless, Marian and I looked there, as we had that very first night I had rescued him, and shelf by shelf we pulled out and down and then looked behind almost every volume. We found nothing.

"Have you really scoured the closets?" Marian asked. I told her that I had. I reminded her that we had looked in every closet at least twice. Nonetheless, she was determined to do it once more. And this time, when she came to the last one, she asked me if I had looked on the very topmost shelf. By now I was so discouraged that I hardly heard her. But when she repeated her question, I pointed out that the topmost shelf, which was a good foot over my head, was at least seven feet from the floor, and that Polar Bear could hardly have made that. He was not, after all, a kangaroo.

Nonetheless, as I said, Marian is very thorough. Whether there was any way for him to get up there or not, look she would. We got out the kitchen steps and, from the top one, she literally chinned herself to peer at the back of that topmost shelf. Suddenly her eyes were looking directly into two other eyes.

"Aeiou," he said.

We were never able to figure out exactly how Polar Bear had managed to get up there. But the fact remained that he had. And one thing we were certain of — once there, he knew perfectly well we were going crazy looking for him. And he was determined to teach us, and especially me, a lesson, and one I would not forget.

It was one which, of course, I never did. Nonetheless, at that moment I was so glad to see him that I would have accepted any lesson. Everything was perfect. Monday morning the woman came and took Bouncer. "I have a wonderful home for him," she said, as she came in and I leashed him up and handed him over to her. I told her he deserved it — he was a wonderful dog. "By the way," she asked at the door, "how did he get along with your cat?" I turned my hands back and forth. So-so, I said.

There were, that spring, no more stray dogs. But there was, soon after, a stray cat — or rather a stray kitten. Again it happened on a weekend, and again on a Friday night. But the rescuer this time was a fellow tenant in my own building. He had found the kitten on the sidewalk only a few blocks away.

He knocked on the door. The kitten, a tiny, sandy-furred ball of mischief, was tucked under his arm. "Here," he said, handing her to me, "I've brought Polar Bear a girlfriend." To him apparently, that was that. Didn't he . . . ? I started to ask — but, no, he didn't. "I've got a dog, you know," he said. Oh, I heard myself starting to assure him, that would be no problem. His dog would . . .

It was no use. The man, who was evidently far wiser in the ways of the territorial imperative than I had been, would have none of it. "Oh, no, my dog wouldn't," he said firmly. "Anyway, the kitten would be much happier with another cat." And with that, and a final wave of his hand, he started down the hall toward the elevator.

But the arrival of the kitten, sudden as it was after the departure of Bouncer, did not really cause me the slightest apprehension. On the contrary, being one of the few animal activists having only one of anything — when there were so many needing homes — I welcomed joining the ranks of the multied. And I was absolutely certain that Polar Bear would be ecstatic about the whole thing. With our new tenant there would no longer be any question of the separation of Church and State, or dog and cat. Now there would be just happy togetherness from one end of the apartment to the other.

In this spirit, I rushed the kitten into the living room to meet Polar Bear. Look, I told him, as I put the kitten down beside him, look what's here. Wasn't she, I asked him, making sure to pat them both at once, just wonderful? Now he would no longer be alone and miserable when I was not around. He would have the kind of companionship he needed, every day and every night as well — with one who was not only of his own kind but also one with whom he could talk and play to both of their hearts' content.

Actually the kitten, I noted delightedly, wanted to play right away — and indeed to her heart's content. The only trouble was it was not to Polar Bear's. The new kitten's idea of heart's content was not just to play some of the time, she wanted to play all of the time — indeed, except when she was sleeping or eating, every single second of all the time.

She would move toward Polar Bear and, as quickly as possible, he would move away. If he moved away slowly, she would move forward slowly. If he moved away fast, she would move forward fast. And, when this began to bore her, she would vary the game. She would pretend, when he moved away, either slowly or fast, not to follow. Then, just when he was visibly sighing in relief, she would fly at him and pounce.

It was this variation of her game plan which led me to name her Pouncer. Pouncer was, I was prepared to admit, not the most original of names. In any case, it did not last long, for as I soon realized, the name Pouncer in no way did justice to her aerial skills. By the end of the first day I had amended her name to Kamikaze.

To say Polar Bear tired of their play is an understatement. Indeed it was soon all too apparent that the same Monroe Doctrine which he had enforced so vigorously when Bouncer was around would also be extended, and in no uncertain measure, to the Kamikaze Kitten.

When it was, however, whenever the kitten would give the signal to let the games begin, Polar Bear would move rapidly to take whatever high ground was at hand — the bed or a windowsill if they were in the bedroom, the sofa, the desk, a chair, or another windowsill if they were in the living room. This would, of course, be frustrating in the extreme to Kamikaze. Over and over, towards whatever refuge Polar Bear had chosen, she would leap and fall, then leap and fall again. Finally, when I could stand it no longer, I would pick her up and put her down beside him.

Polar Bear, who had enough problems with the kitten alone, did not, to put it mildly, take kindly to my entrance onto the playing field. Indeed, he would become so cross about it that he seemed totally to forget that I never fussed over Kamikaze in his presence without fussing, at the same time and even more so, over him. There were no more silent "aeiou" 's — now there were silent hisses and on occasion real ones.

I decided it was high time for another talk, and for this I took him to even higher ground — the mantelpiece. I did not want to be interrupted by Kamikaze and I wanted Polar Bear's undivided attention.

I told him that I was prepared, where Bouncer was concerned, to let bygones be bygones. But Kamikaze was, if he would pardon the expression, a horse of an entirely different color. How could he, I wanted to know, extend his stupid Monroe Doctrine to that darling little member of his own species? Was his heart made of stone?

His answer obviously was that, in this case, it was — or at least I took it so because my opening tirade was greeted with ominous silence. I decided to tone down my rhetoric one notch. All right, I told him, I would admit that Kamikaze could seem, particularly from a totally ego-centered point of view, a bit much. But could he not do her and me the courtesy of managing to remember that he too had once been a kitten? What if nobody had played with him? Had he ever even thought of that?

This time his answer was to turn his back on me — a posture I never tolerated during our confrontations, whether he understood a word I was saying or not. Immediately I turned him round. I well realized he might have had a very difficult time as a stray and maybe very little play. I had no wish to rub a raw nerve, and I should not have brought it up. But, going back to my criticism of his behavior, I told him that I was not just faulting his awful foreign policy, I was also faulting his forever taking the short-term view of everything, and his seemingly utter inability ever to take the long-term view of anything. And this time, I warned him, he could be making a very large mistake. After all, this was not a case like Bouncer's of a temporary visit. Kamikaze was going to be with us permanently. All I was really asking of him was merely a modicum of patience. In no time at all, I told him, Kamikaze would outgrow wanting to play all the time. And, even more importantly, in less time than he realized, he would be an old cat and she would be a dignified adult cat who would surely remember how she had been treated by him when she was a kitten. All and all, it behooved him to mend his ways or the day would come when she would ignore him exactly the way he was ignoring her now and it would be a very unpleasant old age for him.

That was the end of our talk, and I really thought I had done a fine job of giving him the big picture and actually diagramming it as best I could without a chalkboard. Nonetheless, the situation after our talk not only grew no better, it rapidly grew worse. The nights were the worst — they were holy terrors. Polar Bear would leap up on the bed and Kamikaze would of course attempt to follow him. I would then have to reach down and pull her up, after which Polar Bear would attempt to jump back down. What it amounted to for me was trying to hold both of them apart, her from trying to start a game and him from running away. And, the moment I relaxed my hold on him, he was off for the living room and, for all I knew, the mantelpiece. Meanwhile Kamikaze would mew piteously to be allowed to follow him. But it was, of course, pointless to put her down, because she would trail him into the living room and just as piteously mew in there.

Finally, after three nights of almost total sleeplessness, I resolved to go back to the drawing board and begin again. The next free time I had I introduced games that the three of us could play together, everything from ball chasing — Kamikaze actually liked to retrieve — to more specialized endeavors in which, while the participants were primarily Kamikaze and me, Polar Bear could either join in or not as he pleased, but in any case would never feel left out. In addition to these efforts, I even stooped to bribery. Carrying Polar Bear, not terribly willing but at least inert, to Kamikaze's vicinity, I would, when I could manage it, try to place his nose right next to her soft fur. I asked him if she wasn't the sweetest, dearest little thing he ever felt.

He clearly did not think so, not even when I would accompany this special togetherness with a special treat of niblets — which, by literally taking them from right in front of her and giving them to him, I made believe were actually coming from her.

It did not work. Polar Bear, as I should have known, was far above this sort of chicanery. He had made up his mind, and no manipulative measure by me was going to change it. On one occasion he actually spit out a niblet. And even when he ate one, his baleful glance gave me to understand that, just as he would not give in to terrorism, neither would he bow to bribery.

I decided to have one last talk with him. I prefaced this by saying that Kamikaze was obviously such a charming little kitten that it would be easy, if that was what he really wanted, to get another home for her. It was now for him to decide. Did he or did he not care if he ever saw her again? Usually, he at least blinked a little during such talks, and thus I could get some kind of answer. But this time his eyes just stared straight back at me. No, he was obviously responding, he did not care if he ever saw Kamikaze again — in fact, as far as he was concerned, the sooner she moved onward, the better he would like it.

My second question was just as direct. Did he want to spend his whole life as an only cat? And before he answered this one, I reminded him that I had asked that question with all that that implied — one who would be much of the time all alone. Was that, I wanted to know, really what he wanted?

This time I could not vouch for any clear answer to that specific question. But I could hardly have missed the sure sign that being an only cat was indeed exactly what he wanted. Polar Bear did not dislike Kamikaze personally, and he certainly would never have hurt her physically — he was far too much of a gentleman ever to strike a lady cat — but he did very much dislike the idea of her. And it was not all a matter of possessiveness about me, either. It was a kind of possessiveness, it was true, but it was, to his way of thinking, not his for me but rather mine for him. Remember, in his view I didn't own him, he owned me, and it was just as beyond the pale for me suddenly to have another cat as it would have been for him suddenly to have another person. In sum, I was the one who had hurt him, not he me.

In the final analysis then, the whole thing really had nothing to do with Kamikaze at all. It was the fact that Polar Bear seemed to sense that she was to be permanent — and that he could not handle. And, irrespective of the whole thing's effect on him, it was patently unfair to Kamikaze. She deserved a home where she could be, if not the big cheese, at least one in which the big cheese would give her a better break than she had with Polar Bear. In the end I had only one course of action left. I passed the word that I had a kitten for adoption, and I did not hesitate to add to this word the further word that the kitten was, bar none, the darlingest one with which I had ever had anything to do.

When, a couple of days later, a young girl came to pick her up, the girl was, as I knew she would be, totally enchanted — so enchanted, in fact, that when she finally looked up from hugging Kamikaze, she regarded me with an accusing eye. "How on earth," she demanded, "can you bear to give her up?"

I told her that I did not want to, that if it had been up

to me I would have kept Kamikaze forever. But I told the girl I had to — it was a matter of policy. The girl looked blank. I informed her that it was a long story but perhaps the simplest way to explain it was that it was a policy I could do nothing about. It was, I concluded, as if I were in an army, and it was the policy of my superior officer.

The third stray that summer arrived early one June morning via an animal rescuer I vaguely remembered having seen before but could not immediately place. In any case, she had whatever she had rescued right with her in a cat carrier. Oh no, I told her, when I saw the carrier, not another cat. Polar Bear doesn't . . . "No, it's not a cat," the woman interrupted, as she opened the carrier for me, and I tried to peer inside. "His name is Herbert," she informed me. "He's beautiful, isn't he? See, he's lavender."

Actually I could see very little inside the carrier but I saw enough to see that Herbert was, of all creatures, a pigeon — and a very perishable-looking pigeon at that. Right away I remembered who the woman was — one of New York's legendary "pigeon women" — those who befriend the city birds who are so often friendless. I admired her and made an effort to restrain both lack of enthusiasm and incipient sarcasm. I did tell the pigeon woman that I really wondered, having been through a retriever and a kitten, if a pigeon was not just what Polar Bear and I really needed. "Oh, you don't have to worry about that," she said firmly. "I have cats and I've often had pigeons with them."

In that case, I wondered, why had she not had her cats with this one. I did not, however, say so. Instead I asked her what was the matter with Herbert.

The pigeon woman explained that the matter with Herbert was his left wing. She thought he had been hit by a car, she said, but whether he had or not, he would certainly have been hit by one soon if she had not removed him from the street. Herbert, she told me, would try to fly on one wing, but that with his very wounded other one he could not even flutter enough to get away from anything — not, for example, from her when she had gone to pick him up. She had, she said, carried Herbert home, put him in a carrier, and taken him right to the vet. The vet had done a fine job on the wing and had told her that what the pigeon now needed was R&R.

I did not need to hear the bottom line, but I was to do so anyway. "I thought the ideal place," she beamed, "would be your balcony."

You mean, I corrected her sternly, Polar Bear's balcony. My balcony was not wired in.

It was no use. Pigeon women and for that matter pigeon men are probably the most determined of all animal people. In no time at all I was following her — reluctantly — through the bedroom and to the window to the balcony. But, before arriving there, I pushed past her and reached in and removed Polar Bear, who, as we approached, was contentedly taking his morning sun. Although he did not like being ushered out and indeed did not, as he did not to all strangers, take to the pigeon woman, he was soon safely removed and replaced by Herbert.

As the lady busied herself in getting Herbert pigeon food she had brought with her, and building Herbert a makeshift nest out of a bath towel, I noticed that Polar Bear was watching intently from behind his only access route, the firmly closed window. At any moment I expected him to bat at the window, but he did not — in fact he showed, for him, remarkable restraint.

I put it down, however, not to discipline but to patience. I told the pigeon woman that I knew exactly why he wasn't making more of a fuss — what he was thinking was that what she was doing was preparing his lunch. Squab, I elaborated. Not exactly under glass, but close enough to it — behind glass.

The pigeon woman did not think that was funny. "You really don't believe they can be friends, do you?"

I told her I really did not. "You don't know much about pigeons, do you?" she pursued. I admitted to that charge also, but I told her I knew a great deal about Polar Bear. I told her that the day might come, and I really hoped it would, when the lion would lie down with the lamb, but that when the day came when Polar Bear would lie down with Herbert I would, if she would pardon the expression, eat it.

I also reminded her that, before the coming of Herbert, when Polar Bear was in residence in his balcony, other pigeons seemed to like nothing better, knowing that Polar Bear was safely enclosed behind wire and could do nothing about it, than to parade up and down in front of him and, indeed, as close to him as possible. I told her that this behavior would drive Polar Bear into a frenzy — he would crouch, lash his tail, and even leap toward the wire — but now that the tables were reversed and Herbert, not Polar Bear, was the prisoner, surely she could not expect Polar Bear, under these new circumstances and given his previous tormenting, to observe the Geneva Convention.

The pigeon woman did not agree. And, during the next

few days, while she came and went and I looked after Herbert, following the instructions with which I was plentifully provided, I saw no reason to change my mind.

In the times when she was around, I learned a great deal about pigeons. Among other things I learned that they were indeed remarkable birds. And not the least remarkable thing about them was that they and doves were, in reality, the same bird, that both were monogamous and usually mated for life. "I was sure I saw Herbert's mate," the woman told me, "watching me when I picked Herbert up. When he gets well, I'm going to take him to that exact same spot to let him go. Maybe she'll still be there."

The pigeon woman also informed me that pigeons were extremely bright birds, so bright, indeed, that they actually recognized people on the street and that this recognition was accorded not only to people who fed them, but also to people who were just nice to them, and even those whom they simply habitually just saw in a given area. She told me that to her one of the saddest things about them was that, because of the large numbers of pigeons, people almost never paid any attention to them as individuals.

Herbert, I could see for myself, was indeed an individual. He soon became very affectionate toward me as well as his rescuer, coo-cooing cheerfully when I came around and being friendly in his way whether I was coming to feed him or not. Although he spent most of his time in a hunched-up position, with his little head and almost nonexistent neck tucked into his body, as he began to feel better I noticed that he started to change from this position and would sit up, puff out his chest, and preen himself in front of me. One day, the third after he arrived, I found him lying flat on his back on the towel, taking a sunbath.

The pigeon woman was also a mine of information about pigeons as messengers. They could, she told me, fly incredible distances — one, for example, flew from Australia to New York, a distance of over nine thousand miles, and a trip which the bird managed, apparently, by island-hopping. But I was perhaps even more impressed with a World War II pigeon from Fort Meade, Maryland — one which, off on a training mission and becoming thirsty, had flown down to a pond. The pond, however, had been covered with oil, and the bird had become so soaked with it that he could not fly. Several days later, still soaked with the oil and still unable to fly, the pigeon had appeared at Fort Meade. He had walked home — for over one hundred miles.

The pigeon woman's favorite pigeon, however, was one named Cher Ami, the bird which was responsible for saving America's famed "Lost Battalion" in World War I. She told the story extremely dramatically — about how the battalion, surrounded by Germans and low on ammunition, was, as a final straw, being shelled by its own artillery, and its only hope was to get a message back to headquarters to cease the firing. An army major, having just seven pigeons, dispatched them one by one, but all were shot down. Finally the last, Cher Ami, went up. He too was shot and fluttered to the ground. Just before he touched the earth, however, he somehow righted himself and, with one wing shot through and one leg shot off and the all-important message tied to a dangling ligament, reached headquarters. After the war, the woman proudly told me, Cher Ami was awarded the Croix de Guerre by the French government, was sent home by General Pershing in the officers' cabin of a troopship and, later the mascot of the Signal Corps, was buried with full military honors.

By now I was really almost as intrigued with pigeons as my informant, but I still had not the slightest belief that Polar Bear and Herbert could ever be friends. Indeed, as the time went by, Polar Bear seemed to me to get crosser and crosser about the takeover of his balcony and more and more annoyed with me for not at least making an effort to become a white knight. The pigeon woman, however, would have none of such negativism. One day she came in from observing Herbert. "He's almost ready to be let go," she said, "but before I let him go, I want to prove something to you." I started to tell her that the only thing she would prove . . . but I did not even get to my point. As I said, she was a very determined woman.

One thing I insisted on — that at least I be in the balcony when Polar Bear would be allowed to enter. And thus, with Polar Bear still securely in the living room, and the door shut, I climbed out the bedroom window and got into the balcony with Herbert. Still feeling that the whole idea would end in total disaster, I nonetheless resolved to do my best. If I was to be in a United Nations peacekeeping force, I would at least give it the old college try.

At last, sitting directly between the pigeon and the open window, my hands ready to grab Polar Bear, I gave the lady the signal that I was as ready for her idiotic experiment as I would ever be. Listening carefully, I heard her open the bedroom door. The next thing I knew — it seemed less than a second later — I saw a furry whirr fly through the window directly at me. I did not have a chance even to slow it down, let alone grab it.

I am sure that any of you who have read this far could write the inevitable end to the story — of how, in that very next second, both the great experiment and Herbert were terminated and how, conscience-stricken and furious with the pigeon lady, I was forced to bury Herbert, like Cher Ami, with full military honors.

But, if indeed you would write it that way, you would be totally wrong — just as wrong as in fact, although I dislike having to admit it, I was about the whole experiment to begin with. Nothing like that happened at all. Polar Bear leapt past me, all right, using my shoulder as a way station. And then, turning in midair, he landed on Herbert's other side, just as I too spun around in the vain hope of warding off his attack — which was now behind me and would have been much harder for me to thwart.

But no such attack was forthcoming. Polar Bear merely sat down beside Herbert and proceeded to lick himself. Whether he was just glad to have at least part of his balcony back or whether he wanted to make friends with Herbert I could not be certain. Remarkable as was his behavior, however, Herbert's was even more so. Not only did he not move when Polar Bear overflew both me and him, he did not even do so when Polar Bear landed. He kept a beady weather eye on the new arrival — pigeons can see almost directly sideways without moving their heads — but he did not panic, he did not squawk, and he did not try to flutter away. He remained where he was, and for some time the two of them just sat and regarded both each other and the Park down below them, looking for all the world as if they were posing for a new version of *The Peaceable Kingdom*.

"See!" the pigeon woman exclaimed, as she climbed down from the window to be part of her triumph. "I told you so."

I really don't like people who tell me they told me so, particularly when they just happen to be right and I, as I seldom am, just happen to be wrong. And I was glad to see Polar Bear shared this feeling with me. For the fact was the moment the lady got down into his balcony with him, he promptly jumped out again, and took up a watching post on the windowsill.

It was not necessarily, I decided, that he didn't like the pigeon — he just didn't like the pigeon woman. As I told you before, you could never count on his foreign policy.

After Bouncer, Kamikaze, and Herbert, the next order of business on the agenda that summer was a piece of foreign policy of my own — or rather, that of the Fund for Animals. Once more it involved Paul Watson and the Fund's *Sea Shepherd*.

The *Sea Shepherd* had, after the painting of the seals, sailed to Bermuda. From there, Paul called me to ask if I would come down for a meeting. From the tone of his voice, I knew he had another plan.

When I arrived in Hamilton, I soon learned what this plan was — it was to "go after," as Paul put it, the most infamous of the pirate whaling ships, the ironically named *Sierra*. For more than ten years, this ship had broken even the extremely lax rules laid down by the International Whaling Commission, which was then, if not dominated by Russia, Japan, and the other whaling nations, at least rendered largely impotent by them. Operating under various flags of convenience, the *Sierra* had long made a practice of mercilessly harpooning every whale she came upon — mother whales, baby whales, even whales in such declared sanctuaries as the Indian Ocean. She had, among other things, killed virtually every whale around Bermuda.

What, I asked Paul, did he mean by going after her? "I mean," Paul said, "ramming her — putting her out of commission."

I hated the *Sierra* as much as Paul did, but I was taken aback by the idea of ramming another ship. I felt this was stretching animal activism to the limit.

Paul asked me at least to think about it, and that I told him I would do. In point of fact, I thought of little else until we met again — this time in my apartment in New York. Once again, Polar Bear was in on the planning of an operation — just as he had been at the Beverly Hills Hotel when Paul and I had planned the painting of the baby seals. And once again Paul was patting Polar Bear, just as he had been that previous time, while he told me exactly how he intended to do the job.

He pointed out that if we could put the *Sierra* out of commission, it would make it almost impossible for other pirate whalers — there were then five — to get insurance. And that with one blow it was not inconceivable that we could put the entire pirate whaling industry out of business once and for all. "Remember," he said, "we still have all that concrete in the bow — and the rocks."

Once again, as had happened before in our discussion about the seals, it was my turn to pat Polar Bear. I told Paul that I would agree to his plan if he would meet four conditions. I told him I knew he was not big on conditions, but I was going to tell them to him anyway.

My first condition, I said, was that he had to promise me that no matter how the *Sierra* was armed, he would carry no arms, not even a handgun. My second condition was that he also agree not to ram the *Sierra* in the open ocean, but only when she was close enough to the shore so that, if by some chance she sank, and they did not have enough lifeboats on board, or for that matter lifebelts, no one would drown. My third condition was that however he proposed to ram her, he was not to ram her in such a way that the two ships would become stuck together, and her crew could conceivably board the *Sea Shepherd* and injure or kill our crew.

My fourth and final condition was that he, and anybody else on the *Sea Shepherd*'s bridge, have a mattress with them. The *Sea Shepherd*'s bridge was at least forty feet over her deck, and, when the ramming occurred, I believed that the whole superstructure might fall forward to the deck. If they used their mattresses, he and the others up there would at least have the possibility of surviving the fall.

Paul thought about my conditions for a long time. Finally he spoke. "Okay," he said. At the door he picked up Polar Bear. "You know," he said questioningly, "we still don't have a ship's cat."

Taking Polar Bear from him, I told Paul sternly that he still didn't — at least not for that trip.

Early on the morning of July 17, 1979, Polar Bear and I were awakened in the apartment by the telephone. It was a reporter from the Associated Press. He informed me that they had had a report that the *Sea Shepherd*, which they knew was funded by the Fund for Animals, had apparently purposely rammed a whaling ship and did I have any comments?

I told my caller I would have but that first I wanted to

know if anyone had been hurt, and where the ramming had occurred. He told that first reports indicated no one had been injured on either ship, but that the *Sierra* had been badly damaged and that the ramming had occurred about a quarter mile from shore near Oporto, Portugal.

I breathed a deep sigh of relief. Then I told the reporter that, hard as it was for me to condone the ramming of a ship in the open ocean, he must remember that whatever illegality had occurred, it had not begun with us. The *Sierra* had been operating, totally illegally, for ten years and had illegally killed thousands of whales.

Later I heard from Paul the whole story — of how the *Sea Shepherd* had first located the *Sierra* off the Azores and that his crew had wanted to ram her then. But he had remembered my second condition and he had refused. Instead, he had followed the *Sierra* into Oporto, and then, to save our British captain and the British officers, had engineered a kind of voluntary mutiny. He had put the captain and officers off on the dock and then called for volunteers from the crew to go out and do the ramming. In the end, Paul, with just two others, engineer Peter Woof, from Australia, and seaman Jerry Doran from Hawaii, had done the job alone.

And what a job it was! The *Sea Shepherd* had made two runs at the *Sierra*. The first one, at her bow, had sheared off the harpoon and whale-killing gear altogether and then, after bouncing back and negotiating a 360-degree turn, the *Sea Shepherd* had undertaken a second run. This one ran straight at the *Sierra* amidship, and, while her crew scattered either toward the bow or the stern, was strong enough to stave in some fifty feet of her hull and rip open a huge gash in her hold — one which ironically revealed inside her load of illegal whale meat. Even this blow had been, as I had wished, a glancing one. In fact the only condition of mine which Paul had failed to meet was the matter of the mattresses. Paul and Jerry had, as I had requested, brought up two mattresses to the bridge. But when, just before the second impact, Peter had come running up from the engine room, Paul had given his mattress to him.

I forgave him. The *Sierra* never whaled again — nor indeed, shortly afterward because of the insurance cancellations, did any of the other pirate whalers. In the history of the long war to end commercial whaling, the ramming of the *Sierra* was only one battle. But it was a victory — one which, like the painting of the baby seals, had come at a low point in the war. And, widely reported as it was, played a by no means unimportant role in the eventual moratorium on commercial whaling.

As for Polar Bear, for the second time in the brief seven months I had had him, he had brought the Fund, in another extremely high-risk venture, almost incredibly good fortune. And both ventures had, after all, occurred in far-off foreign waters. Certainly for a local land cat, and one with as rotten a foreign policy as his, it was no small achievement.

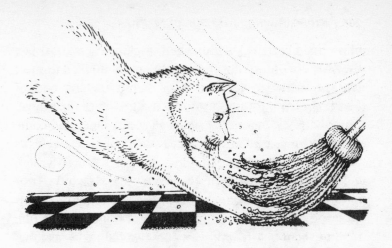

X ○ *His Domestic Policy*

Having addressed Polar Bear's foreign policy toward other animals, I shall now turn, in this final chapter, to his domestic policy — which was in reality his foreign policy toward people. I should like, however, to preface this with the admonitory note that it is one more example that, although Polar Bear and I were similar in outlook in many respects, in this case, as in the one previously discussed about when we were sick, we were two very different individuals.

I, for example, like new people. In fact my critics have been known to say that I am better with new people than I am with other people.

This is not entirely true, of course. My critics are prone to exaggeration and leaping to conclusions and not getting their facts straight. Actually I consider myself second to no one I know at being very fond of certain old friends who are good listeners and are not people who are constantly interrupting me. But at the same time I am prepared to acknowledge that there is, on the side of the critics, something to be said. As fond as I am of any of some of those friends I just cited, I am also extremely partial to almost all new people.

And why, may I ask, should I not be? After all, when you come right down to it, there is a great deal to be said for new people. You can, to begin with, tell them all your old stories without worrying whether or not you have told them to them before, and you can also tell them, as long as you can remember the punch lines, your old jokes.

Besides this, with old friends, even when you are just making polite conversation, you have to rack your brain every other minute worrying, when you ask them a question, whether or not you asked them that same question the last time you met them, or, when they asked you some question, what you answered at that time, particularly if it was something you didn't want to answer to begin with.

On top of it all, you have to remember their names and do so right off the bat — otherwise they will be offended. And even if you can come up with the name, which is by no means always possible, then you also have to remember the names of their damn wives. With new people, you're not expected to remember their names — after all, you just met them.

Finally, with old friends it is sometimes very difficult to convince them that you know more about whatever subject is being discussed than they do. One or the other of them, for all you know, may actually turn out to be an expert on the thing, and, worse still, the kind of expert who has the gall to challenge even your most basic credentials to be one. With new people, on the other hand, you can be an expert on any subject you please — who's to say you're not? — and you can just hold forth and impart your wise counsel, and, because you have just met and there is a certain politeness to be observed, you can do so without ever having the slightest fear of being convicted on some minor fact or date or something which has nothing whatever to do with the strong points you are making. All in all, other things being equal, it can't help but make for a far more interesting discussion — when it's your job to do the talking and it's their job to listen and learn.

Polar Bear, unfortunately, was never able to have this kind of satisfaction because he had never had, if I do say so, my gift of gab. Besides this, as I have said before, he didn't like anything new — and at the top of his list of new things he didn't like were new people.

The fact is he had a totally blind spot about them. Whoever they were and no matter under what circumstances they met him, he was always making one of those ridiculous unilateral decisions of his about them. The basic trouble, I always felt, was that he was simply not up to making any sensible assessment of just what was the difference between new people and people he knew. I could tell him until I was blue in the face that, if only he would give them half a chance, new people would become people he knew. But I was wasting my breath.

There were times, I admit, when the whole thing about new people and him was so frustrating that I more than once envied the person who, instead of having a cat like Polar Bear around, had, perhaps, a dog. Compared to Polar Bear, your average dog is, with new people, the emcee of the Miss America Pageant. Such a dog will run out and greet the new person as if what the dog wanted most in life was to meet either him or her. And that person, of course, will be immediately and highly flattered. And he or she will probably stay that way — particularly if you add to what the dog has done by saying the line so many dog owners are prone to say, that they've never seen that dog that way about anybody before. It is a line which I have often thought should, because of its obvious phoniness, stick in the craw of the dog owner, but it rarely does. As for the new person, because of the general conceit of people regarding their ability to attract any animal's affection, he or she will almost usually swallow it whole. And as for you as the dog's owner, you will right away have the new person eating out of your hand — at the same time, it goes without saying, your dog will soon be eating out of his or hers, and probably something that is very bad for him too.

But no matter. The cat person, or at least a person who is owned by a cat like Polar Bear, has no such easy row to hoe. Not for him is there the remotest possibility that his cat will serve, with a new person, as any kind of icebreaker or even a topic of conversation, let alone one who will become a lasting friend — and all for the simple reason that your cat will be nowhere around.

When, for example, a new person would enter my apartment, the first thing Polar Bear would want to do is to know what possible excuse whoever it was could have for interrupting him at such an hour — and for him such an hour included, of course, all twenty-four. The second thing he would want to know was if there might be anything in the outrageous disruption of his routine which could conceivably be of a positive nature where he was concerned — someone, for example, who might be going to sit down and have, say, with a cup of coffee or a drink, something to eat which would give him a chance for a snack. But this possibility was, in his mind, invariably far outweighed by the negatives — that the new person would be someone who was either loud, hearty, and boisterous and would take entirely too much interest in him, or else someone who had come to take me away from him.

No matter who it was, particularly if it were someone who was going to stay any length of time, Polar Bear wanted equal time to observe them and make up his mind about them. While he was doing this, his two favorite observation posts were, if the person was in the living room, under the sofa, or if the person was in the bedroom, under the bed. And make no mistake about it, he would get to either of these posts posthaste — not only long before they did but also before they had ever seen him.

I am well aware, having mentioned the bedroom, and having already said that I am a bachelor, what some of you are probably thinking — that in such a situation, Polar Bear might be something of an impediment to some romance or other. But I shall not, I assure you, dignify such thoughts of yours in this delicate matter by stooping to give them any answer at all. I shall, however, state only that this is a family book and you should, while reading it, mind not only your manners but your mind as well.

But, to proceed. If a new person did indeed stay any length of time, there was always the possibility that he or she would, sooner or later, spot Polar Bear — at a time when either he partially appeared or else perhaps, from his hiding place, had decided to go to another room or to his balcony. At such times it behooved me, as indeed it behooves any person owned by such a cat in such a situation, to have a veritable litany of excuses ready for recital. One of my favorites has always been "He's a little shy with strangers" — albeit I have found it to be singularly inappropriate on such an occasion as, when for example, Polar Bear had been under the sofa and then would emerge, literally, right beside the newcomer's feet, and scoot like a streak as far away as possible. In any case, others I have used are almost anything to do with the vet, such as "He's just back from the vet" or "He's just had his shots" or even the general "He hasn't been well." Besides these, I also favor an excellent all-purpose one, which is "He's just not himself today."

At first I used to think Polar Bear's attitude toward new people was due to the fact that he had been a stray and had had bad things done to him by people and that therefore he was suspicious of anybody who hadn't proved themselves to him. But I soon learned that this was not necessarily true. Rather it was just a characteristic of, not all, but some cats — and this whether they are purebreds or whatever. We, for example, have had two strays right in the Fund for Animals' office for some years before Polar Bear came. One of them is a beautiful green-eyed coalblack cat who was found, as a kitten, in the lower branch of a tree in the New Jersey woods during a thunderstorm, with none of the rest of her family anywhere around. We called her Little Girl, although this turned out to be, as she grew older, a singularly inappropriate name — for reasons I shall not mention because she is sensitive about it. In any case, Little Girl is as awful as Polar Bear about new people. Whenever she is around and anybody she has not seen before comes into any one of our offices, the next thing you know, she is not only not around, she is not to be found anywhere. The other stray, however, is a large black-and-white male who looks like a tuxedo and should have, in my opinion, been named Tuxedo. Unfortunately, I was overruled, and somebody else, who shall be nameless, decided that his name should be Benedict.

In contrast to Little Girl, Benedict is the soul of friendliness. He welcomes all newcomers to the Fund office as if he were the official greeter, and once they have stated their business and he has escorted them to whichever office they were heading for, the next thing they know, he is in their lap. Benedict is particularly in his element when there are a lot of people around, as at a board meeting, a Christmas party, or even a press conference. If, for example, there is television at the press conference and he has not been invited to appear, he simply waits until the red light goes on and then jumps up into the lap of whoever is on camera. People get to be stars on television by different routes — Benedict knows the shortest, and best.

Benedict particularly likes making friends with people who do not like cats. At one time we had a bookkeeper who admitted he was scared to death of them. Benedict had apparently given some thought to the problem and had come up with a solution. One day he watched, well hidden, while the man, seated in one of the offices and attempting to do his work, was at the same time nervously keeping a lookout for him. Benedict outwaited him and, when the man eventually relaxed his vigil, he crept in from behind his chair, shot up and leapt into his lap. He had apparently decided that the cure for the fear of cats was, like hiccups, a matter of a good surprise.

At first we were ready to scratch one accountant. But this turned out not to be necessary, because, as he so often is, Benedict was right. From that time on, the bookkeeper made his peace with cats. As for Benedict, to this day he continues to like everybody — with one exception. And that is Little Girl. But then, even with the friendliest of cats, you cannot have everything. They are, after all, cats.

The irony of Polar Bear was that, with people he already knew, he was as friendly as Benedict. With Marian, for example — he was extraordinarily affectionate — he would sit on her lap for hours at a stretch, and even when she had to join me in doing something which to him was unforgivable — such as helping me give him a pill — he would afterwards, and in no unmistakable manner, take it out on me but, pointedly, never on her.

There were other people of whom he was also genuinely fond. Most of these were other animal people who either stayed at my apartment when I was away or came in and looked after him when both Marian and I were away. One of his particular favorites was Alex Pacheco, who had crewed on the *Sea Shepherd*, and, although he had not yet founded People for the Ethical Treatment of Animals, was already distinguished as one of the up-and-coming young activists who would shortly revolutionize the animal rights movement. Another was Jeanne Adlon. Jeanne was a former office worker of ours who loved cats so much she soon had a whole business of just looking after them when their regular persons were away. How she did it I never knew, but she sometimes managed as many as twenty calls a day, during which she not only fed each cat on her rounds, but stopped and played with them.

Polar Bear made little trouble too about my chess-playing friends, even when a new one would arrive. Polar Bear was ambivalent about chess. He saw some virtues in it, such as the lack of noise associated with it and also that it usually involved only one other person besides me — which, second to no one, was his favorite number. But there were also two things he did not like about chess. One was what, to him, was the interminable length of it, the other the ridiculous seriousness with which people took it. When, for example, he had a rush call for an appointment on the windowsill to see a pigeon, or some equally important errand — and the shortest way to his destination was directly over the board — he never could understand why everybody made such a fuss about a few little pieces being knocked to the floor, particularly since they were pieces which he knew from experience didn't roll around very well and didn't have anything even remotely interesting, like a bell, inside them.

Other than these people, however, I can count on the fingers of one hand the new people whom, from the beginning, Polar Bear really liked. One was my granddaughter, Zoe. When Zoe first arrived, however, she did so with both my daughter, Gaea, and her husband, Sam, and since this made three people and Polar Bear's outside limit was two, he immediately repaired to his post under the bed. Whereupon Zoe promptly climbed right down there after him and pulled him out — and, to my amazement, he seemed to like it.

The other was Caroline Thompson, a producer and personal friend who had gone with us to Canada to paint the seals. Late one night when I was away, Caroline came to meet Polar Bear for the first time and spend the night there. The next morning, when she had gone and I had returned, I saw that Polar Bear was still asleep. And, when he woke up, he did something I had never seen him do before. He rolled around with an idiotic smile on his face.

Sometime later I was able to figure out why Polar Bear had been so immediately attracted to Zoe and Caroline. With Zoe, I put it down to the fact that she was, at that time, just four years old and was hardly bigger than he was. With Caroline, it was a sterner story. She had gotten him hooked on catnip. I called her immediately and reminded her that Polar Bear was a minor and that she could go to jail for what she had done. I told her I had decided, however, not to press charges. All I was going to do, I told her, was to send him, at her expense, to Betty Ford's.

Ironically, not the least interesting part of Polar Bear's domestic policy was his policy toward a domestic — Rosa, whom we have met before when discussing his diet. In any case, from the moment she first saw Polar Bear, Rosa loved him. She made a great deal of fuss over him and he, in turn, made an equal amount of fuss over her. He made so much indeed that he would permit her to clean and wash and mop and dust virtually anywhere. Not only would he not object, he would happily follow her around and take as much part in her activities as he could. He would even allow her to move him off the bed when she made it, and he particularly enjoyed, as a sort of game, making her also move him off the piled blankets and bed sheets before she remade the bed.

There were, however, two of Rosa's operations at which Polar Bear drew the line. And it was because of these, at least when she was actively engaged in them, that he immediately demoted her again to new person. One of these operations was carpet sweeping, and the other vacuum cleaning. When Rosa brought either of these machines of mayhem out of the closet, it was, for Polar Bear, the signal that diplomatic relations had been broken off and that the lights were going out all over the apartment. War was in fact already in progress and, the moment Rosa turned the machines on, these were, to him, no longer just machines but tanks which had crossed the border. The invasion had begun and he was Rome against the Visigoths, the Allies against the Central Powers, the U.S. against Russia, or simply us against them.

He did not like the carpet sweeper. He did not like the idea of it, or the way it moved. But with it, at least, first running in front of it and then moving to the side to swipe at it with his paws, he had a chance to slow it down and in any case it was reasonably quiet. The advance of the vacuum cleaner, the big tank, was something else again. He purely loathed it. The noise was ear-splitting and it was no longer a fair fight. His only hope was to rip open the bag and get at the infantry inside, but with Rosa constantly moving away from him and at the same time yelling at him above the din, it was all but impossible. He could not hear, of course, that all she was saying was *"Pobre Oso Polar! A tí no te gusta el aspirador, verdad?"* All he heard were command shouts above the noise of the battle. To him, the vacuum symbolized the full horror of modern war, and now it was no longer a matter of just *Amerika* on television. It was a case of infidels in his lair.

On occasion, at lunchtime, I would come home and, if I happened in during the middle of the war, neither Polar Bear nor Rosa would at first notice me, and I would watch the proceedings in amazement. Finally she would see me — Polar Bear was much too busy — and then, of course, she would stop the vacuum cleaner. It was at this time Polar Bear's turn to notice me, and he would run over and give me a terrific welcome. To him, I was the Home Guard, the Seventh Cavalry, the Marines. And I had come up just in time to save the day.

Afterward, however, when Rosa would of course continue with her vacuuming, and when I would obviously be doing nothing to stop her, the whole thing was now, in Polar Bear's eyes, a totally different story. He could not believe I would just sit there. This time I was not merely a traitor, I was far worse — I was someone who, with the war all but won, had snatched defeat from the jaws of victory — who, for some unaccountable reason, had shown the white feather. He would fight on to the bitter end and his inevitable defeat, but, after it was all over and the armistice declared, it would be a long time before he would have anything to do with me again.

As it happened that first summer, I was away from him much of the time because the Fund had begun a domestic war of its own — one which would last for many years — with, of all adversaries, the National Park Service. It broke out first in the Grand Canyon, specifically over the wild burrows there, which we wanted to rescue. To that end we had placed the down payment on a property in Texas, one which I had named after the book which was my favorite as a child. I called it the Black Beauty Ranch, and, though it was at the time small, it at least gave us a place from which, after we had rescued the burros, we would be able to adopt them. The sign at the gate said "Home of the Abused and Unwanted Equine" — but it also had, under this, a quotation from the last lines of *Black Beauty* — "My troubles are over, and I have found a home."

The burros in the Grand Canyon were not the mules which take visitors down to the canyon's floor. Rather they were burros which had been running wild in the canyon since Gold Rush days. The prospectors, not having found gold, had often simply abandoned their pack animals, and through the years their numbers had grown. Before we began our rescue, the National Park Service authorities had estimated their number at between 250 and 300. Actually, as we were soon to learn, government figures were rarely accurate, and there were 577.

At the same time, these same Park Service authorities had in their hands a report from a wildlife biologist which stated that the only answer to the problem of too many burros in the canyon was to shoot them. We were, of course, accustomed to the fact that wildlife biologists in general believe that the answer to almost anything is, if you have a problem, shoot it. But what made this report especially infuriating was that we were told it had been prepared by the same man who was also going to be paid to do the shooting. That was too much — and we were determined to do something about it.

We well knew, to begin with, that the burro is a very difficult animal to shoot. For one thing, he is an extremely intelligent animal, and the minute the shooting starts, he can be counted on to find every possible hiding place in particular in a terrain far more familiar to him than to his prospective killers. For another thing, he has only two vital areas — his brain and his heart — and the gunners, who obviously had little experience with either, would certainly wind up wounding many more burros than they would kill outright. A friend of mine had personally witnessed one burro shoot in which he saw, he told me, "one burro who had ten bullets in him trying to die."

In the century and a quarter the burros had been in the canyon, a number of removal operations had been tried.

All had, for one reason or another, failed. The Fund was determined that ours would not. To begin with, we put together a roundup team which included cowboys, horses, specially trained dogs, and even, ironically, mules — which, since their fathers were donkeys, were smarter than horses and could be counted on not to fall on the perilous rocks and ridges. The team was led by a man named Dave Ericsson, who was not only a world-class roper, but who, I was assured by one of his men, had once roped a rabbit. This was later confirmed by Ericsson himself, who told me, I was certain to reassure me, that he had not hurt the rabbit.

Besides this team, we also decided not to try to herd or lead the burros up the seven-thousand-foot climb to the canyon rim — a tactic which had been previously tried and had invariably ended in failure. Instead we were determined to fly out every single animal — in slings under helicopters.

The first day of our rescue was almost the last. We had been promised by the park authorities that we could use the main, relatively wide, tourist trail to get our team to the canyon floor. At the last moment, the Park Service reneged on this promise and gave us an alternate trail which, in some places, was nonexistent and in others straight down. Still within sight of the top, two horses slipped and several others started to panic — only incredibly quick thinking on the part of our lead riders saved them, and our rescue.

That first day too the temperature at the bottom of the canyon was over one hundred degrees — so high that even if we had found a burro, which that first day we did not, we could not in that heat have, without danger to the horses as well as to him, either rounded him up or roped him. And, even if we had done so, we could not have flown him out — the helicopter, in that heat, would not have had enough lift.

We learned to work in the early dawn hours, when it was cooler, and as late in the afternoon, before dark, as possible — and, one by one, the burros started to come out. At the beginning the cowboys had a lot of fun with the "Bambi-lovers," as they delighted in calling us. One day, at the end of the first week, however, when I had come from another part of the canyon, I noticed a group of them standing around the helicopter. As I came closer I saw that they had that day, for the first time, captured both a mother and a baby burro. I also learned that a spirited debate was in progress about this — one which concerned whether the mother or the baby should be lifted by the helicopter first.

One cowboy was adamantly insisting that it would be better to lift the baby first. The mother would then, he said, at least see what was happening and would be relieved when the helicopter returned for her. Another cowboy, on the other hand, was equally adamant that the mother be lifted first. That way, he said, she would at least know she wasn't being hurt, and that maybe her baby wouldn't be either. Finally it remained for Ericsson himself to settle the matter. First he asked the helicopter pilot what was the heaviest male burro we have lifted so far. "One was close to six hundred fifty pounds," the pilot replied. Ericsson next asked the weight of the heaviest female burro he had carried. "About four hundred pounds," came the response. "Okay," Ericsson said, "how much does a baby weigh?" "I'd say a hundred fifty," said the pilot. "Hell," said Ericsson, "let's build two slings and lift them together."

Our Bambi-loving had, apparently, spread. In any case, it was, we were told, the first helicopter rescue in animal history when a mother and baby had been lifted together. As the summer had waned, and the canyon had cooled, our rescue had speeded up, and we had begun to pick up burros of all sizes, shapes, and colors. One of them, in fact, was white — the first of that color we had seen. He was also a young burro with very much a mind of his own. For me, he was the easiest of any to name. I called him Polar Burro.

Back at the ranch, or rather back at my apartment, there was a problem. It had all come about because of something I had noticed that spring when we had had our first bad thunderstorm. Polar Bear had been terribly frightened. He had had an equally bad time on the Fourth of July, when there were all sorts of fireworks going off in Central Park. These lit up my entire apartment and made so much noise that he was convinced it was, if not the Second Coming, at least the opening of a second front. But a thunderstorm was, to him, even worse. Long before it began, or even I, as an old salt of much rough-weather experience, could see any signs of a storm coming, I would know there was one brewing somewhere because Polar Bear would disappear. Then, when the storm actually did break, nothing I did could comfort him. I could take him as far from any window as possible, to the farthest reaches of the kitchen closet, I could shut the closet door to shut out as much of the audio and video special effects as possible, and even cup my hands around his little ears. But it was to no avail. At best he went totally rigid, and at worst berserk.

One of my friends, who had stayed with Polar Bear when Marian and I were in the Grand Canyon and who had experienced a thunderstorm with him, told me in no uncertain terms when I came back that I would have to do something about the situation. She suggested a cat psychologist.

Before I had had Polar Bear, I had never met a cat psychologist. I had met animal behaviorists, who gave your pet obedience training, or who got him or her over bad habits. But a psychologist who would refine the discipline just to cats — that was, for me, a new experience. I told my friend that if such a person existed and he thought he was going to put Polar Bear through analysis or something like that, he should have another thought coming. I could see Polar Bear analyzing him, but not the other way around.

But my friend, like the donkeys I had been working with in the canyon, would not take no for an answer. "In the first place," she said, "it isn't a he, it's a she. And in the second place, I have already told her about Polar Bear and thunderstorms, and she is ready and willing to handle it."

I was still reluctant. I told her that I was brought up in Boston and the Bostonians I knew didn't put a lot of stock in analysis and psychiatry and all that sort of thing. Frankly, I told her, we thought it was for other people rather than for us — perhaps, I added solemnly, to make other people more like us. My friend just looked at me. Nonetheless, I promised her that if she would give me one last chance to take care of the problem myself, then, if it didn't work, I would agree to seeing the psychologist.

As I had done so often before, I repaired to my growing cat library. In *Your Incredible Cat*, by Dr. David Greene, I came upon something hopeful. Perhaps I could cure Polar Bear of his fear of thunderstorms by ESP.

The first thing I had to do was, apparently, to find out if Polar Bear was right-pawed or left-pawed. "If your cat is left-pawed," Dr. Greene stated, "the chances are good that he possesses psychic ability." Dr. Greene didn't tell me how to do this, but with my usual inventiveness I decided to have a game of ball with Polar Bear and see if he swiped at it more with his right paw than with his left paw. I threw the ball ten times. There were six left-paw swipes and only four right-paw swipes. I was elated. There was no question but that we were on our way. Now the only job left was how to transmit my pro-thunderstorm message to his anti-thunderstorm mind. Dutifully I read on about how I was to transmit and he was to receive. I was apparently, according to Dr. Greene, to do this when he was sitting, not lying down:

> His front legs should be completely straight with his hindquarters placed firmly on the ground. In this position he is most likely to be reasonably relaxed but still sufficiently alert to pick up a telepathic message. He should be facing away from you, with his head turned between 90 and 120 degrees, making it impossible for him even to glimpse your expression or posture, both of which could provide clues which would interfere with the test.
>
> If the cat is looking in the wrong direction, shift your own position rather than attempting to move him, since this inevitably increases his alertness and research suggests that an aroused cat is far less receptive to ESP signals than a relaxed cat.

I did my best. It was awfully hard for me to get him facing away with his head turned between 90 and 120 degrees — I am really no mathematician — but the way I handled it was with the same inventiveness I had used on the left-pawed thing. I got him near the window where he could see pigeons. He was terrific, he never looked at me once.

The second step was, I realized, entirely up to me:

Sit down, make yourself comfortable, unwind physically and clear your mind. Let your thoughts dwell on some pleasantly tranquil image, perhaps a quiet country scene or a soothing color. At first you may find it difficult to banish distracting ideas from your mind, but this will come with a little practice.

Once you feel mentally and physically at ease, glance at your watch to obtain the starting time and then stare hard at your cat for exactly ten seconds. It is essential not to make any movement or sound at this stage to avoid attracting his attention by other than telepathic means.

Focus your mind as intensely as possible on some shared and pleasurable experience, a friendly game or a session of affectionate petting, which you both enjoyed.

Actually what I focussed on was the opposite of a thunderstorm — a nice, sunny day on the balcony playing ball with him. But one day apparently wasn't enough:

Over the next few days or weeks, repeat this test on a further nineteen occasions, varying the time of day at which it is carried out. This is important but investigations have found that ESP seems to be stronger in some people during the evening and more powerful in others first thing in the morning. These changes seem likely to be due to the body's natural, circadian rhythms and the biochemical changes which they bring about in the functioning of mind and body.

I was, frankly, not aware of my circadian rhythms, whatever they were, but I decided to cut down on that idea of nineteen more tests — just a couple more, I felt, would do the job fine.

In any case, at last I was ready to transmit him the message. I beamed it full blast. I told him he wasn't scared of thunderstorms anymore, was he?

I had to wait, of course, for my answer, for the next thunderstorm. Unfortunately, there didn't seem to be any thunderstorms for quite a while. When, finally, one did come, my answer was loud and clear. Not only was he not any better, he was, if anything, worse. I called my friend and told her about my ESP efforts and I reported the unfortunate results. I told her that Polar Bear no longer even waited for a thunderstorm in New York to disappear from sight. Now he would lowtail it for the kitchen closet if the weatherman said it was raining in Baltimore.

I was, I admitted, ready for the cat psychologist. "Good," she replied; "I'll make an appointment for her to come next Saturday morning." There was a pause. "And by the way, I don't want you to be put off by her. She's not very good with people, but she's marvelous with cats."

The woman, when she arrived, was large and formidable. She was also extremely businesslike. Advancing into the living room, she fixed me with a steely eye. "Where," she asked, "are we?" We're in the living room, I told her. "No, no," she said impatiently. "We. We. Where's the cat?" She was, obviously, one of those "we" women so likely to be found lurking by hospital beds in the wake of uncomfortable operations who delight in asking groggy patients if we would like our orange juice now.

Polar Bear had of course, immediately attendant upon

the woman's appearance, repaired to his post under the sofa. I told her he was right under her legs. "Aha," she said. "Well, I don't need us right now. The first thing I would like to do is talk to you, then I will talk to us, and then finally I will want to talk to you both together." She paused and looked down again. "With us out," she added.

I told her it sounded a lot like a divorce or something — that I didn't want to get a divorce from Polar Bear, all I wanted was for him to get over how he felt about thunderstorms.

"As you perhaps know," she said, "I am a structural psychologist. Are you familiar with the work of Dr. Watson?" I told her only through my acquaintanceship with Sherlock Holmes. She ignored this. "Well, it doesn't matter," she continued. "What he believed is that by introducing the verbal report method, he would be able to deal with such common mentalistic phenomena as thinking and feeling — which of course, up to him, had always been in the stronghold of our structural psychologists."

I nodded. "What I will be trying to do," she continued, "is to combine his discipline with my own discipline. And what we will basically have to do here is to decide between an adjustive adjustment and a non-adjustive adjustment, because what we basically have here is clearly a situation neurosis which is undoubtedly induced by a traumatic response which results from a personality disturbance in childhood — or rather, I should say, in kittenhood. I understand we were a stray, so you probably don't know much about our kittenhood, do you?"

I told her I didn't. "A character neurosis can," she went on, as if she were addressing a class of particularly backward students, "like a traumatic situation, induce a situation neurosis."

I started to bridle. I told her Polar Bear had a perfectly good character. "Aha," the woman said again. It was clear that "Aha," second only to "we," was her favorite expression. In any case, she suddenly reached into her handbag and brought out a cassette. "This is a thunderstorm," she said. "Do you have a player?" I told her I did. She handed it to me and then got down on her hands and knees. "I want to get our reaction to it," she said. "Do you have a flashlight?" I procured her one, and then before turning on her cassette, I had a clear sense of déjà vu. It was very reminiscent of that Christmas morning with Mrs. Wills peering under the sofa to see whether or not she was going to take Polar Bear away.

The cassette was audio only — like one of those sleep records people turn on to hear gentle ocean noises or soft music, only in this case it was the opposite. Almost at once the room was filled with a booming, roaring din, complete with claps of thunder and even loud crackles, apparently to simulate lightning. At the very first boom, before even the first crackle, Polar Bear bolted. He almost knocked the flashlight out of her hands, crack blocked one of her ankles and then headed full speed for the kitchen closet. "Oh dear," she said, rising quickly and watching him, "we don't like it, do we?" No, I said grimly, we don't. I tried to stop her but she went into the closet after him. She did not, however, catch him. No woman alive — and few male cornerbacks — could have. The next thing I saw was Polar Bear heading for the bedroom, with the woman in full pursuit.

Fortunately, in a moment or two, her thunderstorm was over and I did not have to wait long before she reappeared. "We went out the window," she said, "I saw where we went but I decided not to go down in there after us."

I told her she had made a wise decision — that Polar Bear had gone to his balcony, which he regarded as a sort of refuge, but that perhaps, after he had calmed down, that would be a good place for her to talk with him.

The woman agreed, after making me promise to stay where I was. In a very short time, however, she was back again. "Well," she said, sitting down, "we're not very much of a communicator, are we?"

Once more I bridled. What, I wanted to know, did she expect — Ronald Reagan? I told her Polar Bear was in his way, at least with me, a great little communicator. "Aha," she said. "And how, may I ask, do we communicate with you?" I noted an edge in her voice, but I was firm, nonetheless. We talk, I said.

"We talk?" she questioned. "You mean *you* talk." No, I said firmly again, both of us talk. I talk to him and he talks to me. "You mean, *we* talk to you?" she repeated. This time I detected an even sharper edge.

I told her we certainly did, particularly when I was talking to us about something I wanted us to do and we were talking to me about what we didn't want. To do, I added lamely.

"Mr. Amory," she said quietly, "cats don't talk."

I wanted to say that she had certainly come into the book at a hell of a time to give me that piece of news — but I refrained. Instead I asked her why, if that was true, had she gone out to the balcony to talk with Polar Bear?

"I talked," she said sternly, "we didn't. We don't talk. What we give me are verbal pictures — images, if you will."

Then it was, I said, sort of like television? She nodded. "I've been meaning to ask you," she said, "if we watch television?"

I shook my head and for the first time smiled at her. I said I thought television was maybe too prejudiced for him — that there were all kinds of dogs in programs, and they even had shows of their own, but never cats — that there weren't even cats in family shows. All cats ever got to do was to appear in commercials and sell cat food.

"Do we spend much time in front of the mirror," the woman asked, "looking at ourself?" I told her he did nothing of the sort — that he wasn't at all vain and anyway what he thought he saw in the mirror was another cat. And he didn't like that, because he wanted to be an only cat. The woman picked up on this right away. "You mean," she asked, "he won't tolerate any other cats?" Not very well, I admitted.

"Aha," she said. "And you live alone, I understand." I nodded. "I think," she said, "we're beginning to get to the bottom of this. You know the visual image I got from us out there was a very clear red."

Red? I inquired. I told her I thought all cats were color-blind. She shook her head. "No," she replied. "The latest data suggest that they're not. They see in several colors — and red denotes something very specific."

I wanted to say that if Polar Bear saw red, he was, in my opinion, angry. And why shouldn't he have been? After all, she had turned on a thunderstorm and then chased him out on the balcony, where he never went when there was a real thunderstorm, and then when he got there, he found there wasn't any thunderstorm at all, but she had just made one up.

As I was thinking this, I had missed some of what the woman had been saying, but I came in on the end of it. "The color red," she said, "is usually an indication that what's bothering us has to do with our owner. I want to ask you something. Are you afraid of thunderstorms?" I told her that of course I was not afraid of thunderstorms and that if she thought I had given a fear of thunderstorms to Polar Bear, she was barking up the wrong tree. "You may not have given it to us," she said quietly. "We may have gotten it in our kittenhood. But what you have done is to bring it out and reinforce it."

How had I done that? I wanted to know. "You probably don't realize it," she said, "but you do fear thunderstorms. You fear them if for no other reason than that you know they will make us afraid." I said nothing. The cat psychologist stood up. "Well," she said, "I think that's enough for our first appointment. I've definitely decided we are not going to make an adjustive adjustment. We are going to make a non-adjustive adjustment. The next time there's a thunderstorm, I don't want you to pay any attention to it and above all I don't want you to pay any attention to our reaction to it."

My friend had supplied me with a psychological dictionary and, after the woman had gone, I looked up adjustive and non-adjustive adjustments. I did not understand them but shortly after them I came upon the definition of the "Aha" or "Ah-ha" experience. It was, the dictionary said, "The reaction accompanying the moment of insight in problem solving situations."

It was my turn to say Aha. And my problem-solving with Polar Bear involved one last compromise with him. If he would promise to try to be a little better during thunderstorms, I would promise never to have the cat psychologist back again.

I kept my promise, too. I did not, however, agree to cease and desist from another activity over which Polar Bear and I had constantly warred. This was the simple question of my, upon occasion, throwing a party. Parties were Polar Bear's particular bêtes noires. He could sense a party coming long before the arrival of the nice young couple who would usually be catering it. I have never understood how he did this — whether it was a sudden increase in phone calls, whether it was Marian rearranging furniture and bringing in flowers, or whether it was an extra-long war with Rosa and the vacuum cleaner. Whatever it was, by the morning of the party itself, and the coming of the caterers, Polar Bear was ready to go into his act.

I, of course, was well aware of exactly what was going on in his little hermit's mind, but whether I was or not, it made no difference. He wanted to show me that he was already a nervous wreck, and he also wanted me to know that he held me personally responsible for his condition. In any case, the first thing he did was to let the caterers know he also knew precisely what they were up to, and that it was something up with which he had not the slightest intention of putting. This already irritated me because the caterers were very fond of him and in fact did everything they could to win him over. But he would have none of it — indeed he gave them the strongest insult possible, which was to ignore their blandishments to entice him into the kitchen for an hors d'oeuvre.

Next it was my turn. As the caterers busied themselves in the kitchen, and I sat in the living room giving them helpful advice, he would walk back and forth in front of me, pausing only long enough on each turn to give me a look of withering disgust. "You know perfectly well," he would say, to begin our colloquy, "what happened to me the last time you gave a party."

Having heard the same speech several times before, I would be in no mood to hear it again, and would interrupt what I knew he was going to say next. I did indeed know what had happened to him, I would inform him. He had gone under the bed the moment the first guest had arrived and had not reappeared until the last guest had gone.

It was his turn to interrupt. "I am not talking about where I was fortunate enough to find refuge," he would say. "I am talking about what happened afterwards. You have probably forgotten, but I was at death's door for at least three days."

I told him that he was talking arrant nonsense. He had been in perfectly good health, he had just pretended to be sick because, in his warped little mind, he believed that I had purposely given the party to make him sick.

"And which, whether you know it or not," he would interrupt again — and this time in such a way as to point out that he had not heard a word of my previous statement — "was probably responsible for shortening my short little life."

Whenever he referred to that, I really felt that he was hitting below the belt. I told him that we were not discussing the shortness of anybody's life. What we were discussing, or at least should have been discussing, was that occasionally I gave a party because I happened to wish to pay back the people who had been kind enough to invite me to their parties.

Of course he made no effort whatsoever to understand that. As far as he was concerned, there was no need for me either to be having parties to thank people who had invited me to their parties, or, for that matter, for going to their parties in the first place. Instead, I should have at least the outward courtesy, if I was incapable of any inward understanding, to spend what were probably the last few evenings he had left on this earth in my home, alone, with him.

I would then tell him that I would simply not countenance any more of that self-pitying drivel. I would also add that he was, at most, two years old and should live perhaps ten times that long unless, by his total intransigence, he was determined to induce a wide variety of nervous disorders which could indeed bring him to an untimely end. But, I would warn him, if this did occur, he would be the one responsible, not me.

Finally I told him that for this particular party, I had at the very least assumed that he would take, if not a completely different attitude, at least not such a ridiculous one as he had about my previous parties. It was, after all, the first anniversary of the night on which I had rescued him, and I did feel that on this of all nights I had a right to look forward to something more than one of his infuriating disappearance acts. I admitted freely that there would be some people at the party who might be new to him, but there would be many with whom he was already acquainted — people such as Sergeant Dwork, my brother and his wife, and even Mrs. Wills, who had, in a sense, rescued him in reverse. Besides these, there would be people he knew much better because they had actually stayed with him at the apartment — my daughter, Gaea, my granddaughter, Zoe, Jeanne Adlon, and Caroline Thompson, the catnip provider. There would be even be a couple of his old friends from California, like Paula Deats, who would be coming all the way to New York to celebrate Christmas because they didn't have it out there.

I mapped it all out for him very carefully, and as the first guest arrived, I still had hopes. But by the time the second couple rang the doorbell, these hopes were dashed. Polar Bear had disappeared.

Marian and I devised a system whereby we kept an eye on the door as people arrived and departed to insure that he did not do likewise. And on occasion, and as inconspicuously as we could manage, we surreptitiously peered under the bed, to make sure that he was still there. Unfortunately, my checking was not surreptitious enough to escape the sharp eye of that redoubtable newsman Walter Cronkite. He had come upon me while I was assuming the couchant position by the side of the bed and, with an unerring nose for news, demanded to know what I was doing.

Turning and looking upward, I confessed that I was checking on my cat. Walter loves cats, and at that time had a cat of his own named Dancer — one who had been left with him on a temporary basis by his daughter but to whom he had grown so attached that he had permanently purloined it. "Cat?" he now queried. "You have a cat? What's his name?" And assuming the couchant position beside me, he also peered under the bed. "Hi, Polar Bear," he said coaxingly. "Come here, Polar Bear."

I would like to be able to say that Polar Bear rose to the occasion, but the sad fact is rise he did not. Walter Cronkite might, that very year, have been voted the Most Trusted Man in America by a large majority of the television viewing audience, but to Polar Bear such a distinction signified nothing. He was simply a new person, and Polar Bear backed, if possible, even farther into the farthest wall.

As Walter and I, defeated, rose to our feet, however, we managed to bump into the chessboard, which I had set up in the bedroom and at which Mr. George C. Scott was deeply engrossed in a titanic struggle with an opponent I had especially chosen for him — a young woman who was highly ranked as a tournament player. George, who had met Polar Bear, was suddenly interested and demanded to know where he was. I gestured futilely under the bed. "What the hell do you mean he's under the bed?" George said. "He can't spend the entire party cooped up under there!" And without further ceremony, and in the same famous rasp with which he had roused the Third Army in *Patton*, he gave Polar Bear his marching orders. "Polar Bear," he growled, "come here."

I smiled at George pityingly. Cats, I informed him, don't do that. Dogs do that. George's own dog, the mastiff Max, probably did that. But cats never do it, and certainly not Polar Bear. He simply wouldn't . . .

"He wouldn't what?" George inquired blandly. Because at that very moment, and looking nonchalant in the extreme, Polar Bear had materialized from under the bed. He walked unconcernedly over to George, stretched, and then in front of everyone all but saluted.

It was just one more illustration, if one were needed, that his domestic policy, like his foreign, had its exceptions.

When I awoke the following morning, Polar Bear was standing on the rug beside my bed, regarding me intently. I saw at once that he was not giving me his usual after-party, death's door act. Either he had forgotten to do it or he was, miracle of miracles, actually getting used to an occasional party.

He was, in fact, I thought, standing in almost exactly the same position as he had stood on that Christmas morning one year ago, and he was looking at me in almost exactly the same way. But he was now a very different cat. Instead of the thin and injured and frightened stray who had decided to try his luck with me, there stood a cat who was breathtakingly beautiful, glossy, and fat — well, I amended, possibly portly — and whose soft green eyes gazed into mine contentedly. If my ears did not deceive me, he was purring.

I lay and looked at him for a long moment — and thought of the incredible difference he had made in my life. But then, as I continued to look, his purring stopped. His eyes slowly narrowed and his tail began to twitch. Sentiment was all very well, he was clearly saying, but adult individuals did not wallow in it. Life goes on, parties or no parties, holidays or no holidays, and was I or was I not going to get out of bed and fix him his breakfast? In case I did not grasp his meaning fully, he spoke.

"AEIOU!" he said.

"Aeiou yourself," I replied, as I scooped him up on the way to the kitchen. "Merry Christmas."

○ *L'Envoi*

The events in this book all took place, as I have indicated, during Polar Bear's first year with me. That was, as I write these lines, almost a decade ago.

I am well aware that in most books about individual animals, the animal dies in the end. I have never liked this — indeed that was one of the reasons why, even as a child, *Black Beauty* appealed to me so much. It is true there was misery and suffering in the book. But, in the end, Black Beauty has not died.

Neither, I am happy to say, has Polar Bear. He is very much alive, thank you. In fact neither he nor I even consider him an old cat. When some young whippersnapper comes along, and it is necessary to establish precedence, we may use the word *mature* — but never *old*.

What Polar Bear is today is a senior citicat — with all the attendant rights and privileges that this title implies.

He does not travel on buses for less or see movies at a lower price, but that is only because he does not like to travel at all, and he would not be fond of most modern movies.

In some ways he has become, through the years, as indeed perhaps his biographer has as well, steadily more curmudgeonly. He is very aware, for example, that many changes have occurred in our lives and that not all of them have been for the better. He has seen too many examples of inferior service, unnecessary regimentation, lack of respect for elders, and, in commercials, the everlasting use of kitten and young cat actors who have not learned their craft. But in some of the areas discussed in this book he has, at the same time, become less critical.

One of these is the matter of transient strays. I do not say that he welcomes them wholeheartedly, but at least he has a more philosophical attitude toward them than he had in that first year. Only the other day, for instance, he almost wagged his tail at a dog who was passing the night. It is true that I started the wag, but still he made an effort to complete it.

I have also noted some — repeat some — improvements in his behavior toward new people. If he is particularly comfortable on the sofa, for another instance, and a new person appears, he will very often these days not even bother to bolt down and hide underneath it. I would like to add that I have seen similar improvements in his attitude toward travel, toward diets, toward fitness programs, toward large and noisy parties, toward thunderstorms, and even toward the vacuum cleaner. Unfortunately, that would be paltering with the truth. About all of the above he remains firmly unconvinced.

It might be said that I have made a lot of fun of him

in this book — but then, so has he of me. The fact remains that, in making fun of each other, we have had so much fun together that I hope those of you who have undoubtedly had similar experiences with your own animals will share in it with us.

But I hope even more that those of you who have never had an animal will hie yourselves to the nearest shelter, and adopt one. If you do, you will surely find that that animal will give you, every day of his or her life, not only joy and companionship but also that very special kind of love which can be understood, as I said at the beginning, only by those fortunate enough ever to have been owned by one.

TIME FLIES
by Bill Cosby

"Today, at fifty, I am looking with more interest than ever at the medical researchers, cheering them on to cure everything from hypertension to hives. The average person wonders every day about the weather, but I never think about that. I think instead about when Macy's will be getting artificial hearts.

"Immortality is a long shot, I admit; but *somebody* has to be first."
                    Bill Cosby in *TIME FLIES*

Getting older is no laughing matter, but Bill Cosby's new book will change all that — bringing his unique warmth, wisdom and wit to a subject of even more universal appeal than the perils of raising children. It's all about *time* — and the shifting way we view the world at different stages: at 5, at 13, at 21, and on through the decades from 30 to 60 as the surprises get ruder, the indignities mount and the rewards actually get richer.

Like FATHERHOOD, TIME FLIES is structured around vignettes and anecdotes from Bill Cosby's own experiences, delivered in the hilariously personal and inimitable style that has propelled him to the top of the bestseller lists.

0 553 17517 3

FATHERHOOD
by Bill Cosby

'Comic good sense from Britain's favourite Transatlantic TV funnyman'
DAILY MAIL

When the world's funniest father sits down to write his first book, what better subject could there be than fatherhood itself?
In FATHERHOOD, Bill Cosby's special brand of humour, wisdom, and just plain wonderful humanity come together to create a joyous celebration of being a father.
FATHERHOOD is. . .
pretending that the present you love most is soap-on-a-rope.

◆

knowing that you're in trouble when the child says "No problem".

◆

thinking that the height of fashion is matching socks.

◆

helping your child learn English as a foreign language.

◆

not being the boss of the house because you've seen the boss's job and you don't want it.

0 553 17463 0

THE BOY WHO SHOT DOWN AN AIRSHIP
by Michael Green

In this first part of his autobiography, Michael Green, author of the bestselling *Art of Coarse* books, treats us to an account of growing up in the 1930s and 1940s that is both hilarious and moving. Indeed, it was his adventures as a Leicester schoolboy, as an ill-fated cub reporter and as an accident-prone young soldier learning the facts of life, that inspired the comic series that would later become a household word.

The Boy Who Shot Down an Airship is at times comic, at times nostalgic, the picture of a thirties childhood vividly remembered and the frankest, funniest portrait for years of life in khaki.

'A lovely read. . .these poignant, funny memoirs are his best work. *Treat yourself*'
SUNDAY TIMES

'The Boy Who Shot Down an Airship is funny and nimbly written, but it's the small details of a vanished England that give the book its special flavour'
EVENING STANDARD

'Good "coarse", high-spirited stuff'
PUNCH

0 553 17607 2

THE CHINESE ALMANAC 1990

Day-by-day predictions to guide you successfully through the coming year compiled by Kwok Man-Ho.

What does the coming year have in store for you? Could it bring you rich rewards? Will your lovelife be highlighted? Is it time to change careers? Don't leave anything to chance — let the wisdom of the Chinese Almanac guide you.

Kwok Man-ho, one of the few fortune-tellers able to calculate the almanac using ancient astrological charts and tables, has drawn up this unique edition of the Chinese classic that will show you how to direct your energies towards happiness and success. Packed with predictions and a wealth of advice, this invaluable handbook will help ensure that 1990 is your best year yet!

0 553 17603 X

MOVIES ON TV 1989-90
Edited by Steven H. Scheuer

GIANT NEW 30TH ANNIVERSARY EDITION — THE
BIGGEST EVER!

It's a great era to be watching movies. Now you have access to
more film than ever before, and you can view them virtually anywhere you choose — in the theatre, on regular TV, cable TV, or
on videocassette. But how can you be certain you are making the
right and best choice for you and your family?

THIS IS THE ONLY GUIDE YOU NEED TO HOLLYWOOD'S
BEST MOVIES.

They're all here: the stars, directors, ratings, reviews, and fascinating
inside information. PLUS — A special reference key tells you which
movies are currently available on videocassette.

INSIDE **MOVIES ON TV**

* MOST COMPLETE LISTING OF MOVIES ON VIDEO-
  CASSETTE
* MOVIES LISTED ALPHABETICALLY
* CONCISE PLOT SUMMARIES
* PRECISE, EXPERT REVIEWS
* 4-STAR RATING SYSTEM

From the newest box-office smashes — *Who Framed Roger Rabbit?*,
Coming to America, *Die Hard*, and *The Last Emperor* — to all-time
greats from the past — *Citizen Kane*, *It's a Wonderful Life*, *The
Sound of Music*, *Rocky* — to classic cult 'bombs', they are all here.
More information than in any weekly guide — in one volume!

0 553 268511